The Ultimate Guide to Becoming a Nurse

MA Molesworth

Published by HealthLearn Ltd.

HealthLearn Ltd
272 Bath Street
Glasgow
Scotland
G2 4JR
Website: HealthLearn.co.uk

ISBN: 978-1-7395112-1-0

Images: Cover image, Antonio Carlos Bezerra/iStock.com; Figure 4.1, licenced by the World Health Organisation with retained rights.

DEDICATION

I express sincere gratitude to my family for their unwavering support and enduring patience throughout the process of writing this book.

CONTENTS

	Acknowledgments	i
1	Introduction	1
2	Becoming a nurse	5
3	Choosing a university	32
4	What to do before you start	53
5	The transition	78
6	Achieving success	107
7	Thriving during your studies	144
8	Nursing placements	170
9	Career options	199
10	Conclusion	215
11	References	217

ACKNOWLEDGMENTS

Thanks to Amber for drawing upon her extensive nursing experience to provide ideas and insights that have informed the development of this book. These contributions have helped produce authentic guidance and scenarios designed to benefit anyone interested in becoming a nurse.

INTRODUCTION

We have designed this book to be your guide for navigating the path to an exciting and rewarding career in nursing. Use it as a compass to assist you through each stage of the process. It will help you become familiar with the role of the nurse and succeed in achieving your goals. Whether you are exploring your options or are already on the way to becoming a nurse, this book will offer helpful information and insights. Each path to becoming a nurse is unique and filled with possibilities for personal development and self-discovery. Regardless of your background, you will bring a wide range of experiences and insights to the journey. Nursing will offer opportunities to engage with others and learn more about yourself along the way. The path towards your new future will be intricate and complex, requiring you to become familiar with different processes, academic requirements, clinical skills, and healthcare settings. This book will help you get acquainted with all these areas and more. Use the information and activities provided to help you confidently navigate the landscape ahead.

We have carefully designed each book chapter to demystify the process of becoming a nurse, providing practical advice on securing a spot in a nursing programme, preparing for your studies, and succeeding once on the course. There are specific sections which set out the types of nursing courses available and how to choose the right university for you. You will discover practical considerations, including professional requirements, recommended reading and the equipment that will help you develop your clinical skills. The transition to studying nursing at university can be daunting, so we will tell you what to expect through the journey. We intend to help you understand university structures and hit the ground running when you start your course. This leads into a chapter focused on thriving throughout your studies, a must-read on using support to ensure you excel during your nursing studies. You will learn various strategies for success, which will help you progress and ensure the journey is enjoyable.

Because nursing is a practice-based profession, we include a section on clinical placements. This information will help you establish how to get the most out of your hands-on experiences working with people needing care. It consists of a wealth of insider knowledge and draws on evidence to help prepare you for real-life scenarios. It will help boost your confidence to learn and grow in different settings, learn how to deal with problems, find your voice, and ultimately thrive in your placements. *The Ultimate Guide to Becoming a Nurse* will also help you visualise your end goal by setting out career options and illuminating opportunities you may not have thought about. Nursing is a diverse profession with career paths in patient care across acute and community settings, research, education, and policymaking. This book is a valuable resource and a guide. It will help boost your confidence and inspire you to make informed decisions about your future. It encourages you to ask the right questions and establish meaningful goals to enable you to forge a rewarding and secure future. The following pages provide a mix of practical advice and useful information supported by real-life insight from nurses, nurse lecturers and student nurses. You will hear inspirational stories about the challenges and triumphs of the nursing profession. So now is the time to embark on a journey that will turn your dreams into reality. Pursuing a career in nursing is not about what you do. It is about who you become.

Information and links

Information about fees and funding reflects information available at the time of writing. The figures, eligibility criteria, and other factors regularly change, so we often provide links to the sources of the information. These will enable you to check the most up-to-date details. While all links worked at the time of publication, these can change over time and may no longer take you to the relevant page. In such cases, please try searching for pertinent information via a search engine. If, within one year of purchase, you are unable to follow a link in this book, we are here to help. If you cannot find the required information via a search engine, please email info@healthlearn.co.uk stating the book title, the chapter title and the section title. Please also provide a copy of the link that is not working. We will send you an alternative link if available.

Patient scenarios and student details

Although based on common clinical and healthcare situations, all patient scenarios are fictitious. Any similarity to a specific person or set of circumstances is a coincidence. Where a student nurse's name is referred to within the text, please note that a pseudonym has been used in place of the person's real name to protect their confidentiality.

BECOMING A NURSE

Introduction

Choosing a nursing career is a significant decision that has the potential to transform your life. Embarking on this journey will also result in you positively influencing many other people's lives. Becoming a nurse will be both rewarding and challenging, as fulfilling as it is difficult. Whether you are driven by a lifelong passion or a new calling, each person's route towards becoming a nurse is unique. Either way, it is a step forward into a world of opportunity and growth. This first chapter will take you through the early stages of the process. It will focus on important considerations such as the first step, conducting research, and the role of family and friends. We have also included an open discussion of the pros and cons of becoming a nurse. You will need as much information as possible to make the right decisions about your future. This chapter will help you to become acquainted with the healthcare environment and the different professional options within nursing. It will provide insights into the nursing profession that you will not find in glossy university brochures. Your journey towards becoming a nurse begins here.

The nursing role

Becoming a nurse in the UK requires significant time, effort, and dedication. It is a career choice that will profoundly impact your life, allowing you to build a rewarding future and make an essential contribution to society. An important first step in your journey is to make sure that you understand the role of the nursing role. Nurses are the largest professional group in the UK and are essential to the UK's healthcare system and the population's overall health and well-being. The number of nurses, midwives and nursing associates registered with the Nursing and Midwifery Council (NMC) (2023a) to practice in the UK has grown to a record total of 788,638! During 2022-2023 the highest-ever number of nurses, midwives and nursing associates joined the profession, with more than 52,000 registering. Nurses play a crucial role in society, caring for millions of patients and their families each year. This care extends beyond the clinical duties to include the emotional and communicative aspects of supporting patients.

Nurses often interact with patients more frequently than any other healthcare professional, leading to a deeper understanding of their needs, fears, and hopes. These insights enable them to act as advocates, ensuring patients' rights are respected and their healthcare preferences are recognised (Blackburn, Johnson, Chaveleh, 2020). Advocacy is the act of a nurse supporting the rights and interests of their patients, ensuring their voices are heard within the healthcare system. Nurses often have a central role in coordinating care among various healthcare professionals, including medical staff, physiotherapists, pharmacists, occupational therapists and speech and language therapists.

Nurses look at their patients holistically, taking into account their psychological, social, and spiritual needs. They treat the 'whole person,' providing comfort, empathy, and respect in addition to clinical and medical treatment. Importantly, nurses have a role in educating patients about their health conditions and how to manage them, allowing them to take control of their health (Fawkes and Moore, 2019). They also provide preventative health education, promoting healthy lifestyles and behaviours among individuals and communities. As was evident during the Covid 19 pandemic, nurses are vital to public health initiatives and frequently work in community settings to implement strategies, support vaccination programmes, and help to manage outbreaks. The following section will explain the various fields of nursing in more detail.

Fields of nursing

Your critical next step is understanding the different fields of nursing and considering which one aligns with your career goals. Your decision is influenced by the kind of nursing you wish to pursue during your career. As nursing is regulated, becoming a nurse involves meeting the requirements set out by the NMC, nursing's regulatory body. Its purpose is to ensure that nurses deliver healthcare to agreed standards (NMC, 2018a). The NMC holds a register of all nurses, midwives, nursing associates and nursing specialisms working within the UK. The NMC (2020) recognises four fields of nursing, each with its patient population, type of care, and practice setting. Here is a summary of each:

- **Adult Nurse:** The largest field of nursing, adult nurses usually care for patients over 18. They can work in various settings, including hospitals, clinics, community health centres, and patients' homes. They provide direct patient care, support families, and coordinate services other healthcare professionals provide. Their duties range from performing complex clinical procedures to assisting patients in managing their illnesses and lifestyles.
- **Children's Nurse**: Also known as paediatric nursing, child nurses care for children from infancy to late adolescence. They are employed in various settings, including paediatric hospital units, community paediatric services, and school clinics. Child nurses often help children and families to manage the fear and anxiety they may experience in healthcare settings. They advocate for children's rights and

safety and frequently collaborate with other healthcare professionals and social services.

- **Mental Health Nurse**: Mental health nurses are educated to care for people of all ages who require support for various mental health conditions. Among these are schizophrenia, bipolar disorder, depression, anxiety, and many more. They work in multiple settings, including psychiatric wards, community mental health centres, and community mental health teams in patients' homes. They must establish trusting and respectful relationships with patients and their families while maintaining professional boundaries.
- **Learning Disabilities Nurse**: Learning disability nurses assist people of all ages with learning disabilities to live as independently as possible. They can work in various settings, including community teams, schools, and nursing homes. Their responsibilities frequently include promoting the physical and mental health of people with learning disabilities, providing health education, assisting with daily living skills, and coordinating care. They also collaborate closely with families, carers, and other healthcare and social service providers.

To become a registered nurse in any of these fields, you must complete a nursing degree in the relevant field. The NMC approves universities offering these degrees, and the university will notify them when you qualify so they can add you to the nursing register.

Before applying to start your nursing studies, it is highly recommended that you know which nursing field you wish to specialise in and why you chose it. You will likely be asked about this during the application process -complete Activity 1.1 to help you reflect on which field might suit you best.

Activity 1.1: Fields of nursing

This reflective activity has been designed to help you narrow down the field of nursing that might suit you. Start by viewing the following resources to get an inside look at each of the four fields of nursing:

- ***AdultNursing:***
  https://youtu.be/RWFbnJRwDGA
- ***Child Nursing:***
  https://bit.ly/3YCoEd9
- ***Learning Disability Nursing:***
  https://youtu.be/Co0_VrifKEc
- ***Mental Health Nursing:***
  https://bit.ly/3OuGZnE

Now picture yourself as a nurse from one of the four fields, imagining what your day might be like. Repeat this thought experiment for the other fields writing a few sentences for each. Describe the experiences, challenges and rewards that may come from working with adults, children, people with a learning disability or people with mental health needs. Consider how you feel about each of these scenarios as you imagine them. Do you get more excited about one of the roles than the others? Your personal responses to this activity may provide a helpful starting point for the nursing field that best suits you. As you progress through this book, continue to reassess your feelings and learn more about nursing and the available choices.

Question

- *How might your personal life experiences or interests influence your affinity towards a specific field of nursing?*

A suggested answer is given at the end of the chapter.

By learning about the different fields of nursing, you are now well-placed to continue on the path to success. In the following sections, we will consider the pros and cons of a career in nursing to help you make informed decisions.

Work-life balance and pay

Before beginning a career in nursing, it is helpful to understand both the rewarding aspects and the challenges of the profession. Balancing the pros and cons will give you a more realistic perspective and the necessary information before committing to the next step. This section will discuss the advantages of becoming a nurse, including salary and job satisfaction. Later in the chapter, we will consider the challenges and stresses associated with nursing. In recent years, high vacancy levels have led to a surge in demand for nurses in the NHS. This demand brings job security and employment opportunities across settings and regions. As a future nurse, this will allow you to match your career preferences and personal circumstances to the available vacancies. Recent figures from the Royal College of Nursing (RCN) (2022a) show the vacancy rate of registered nurses is around 46,800. There are also many opportunities to work overseas as a registered nurse, with many countries seeking to attract nurses to work within their health systems. Circumstances can change, but the lack of suitably qualified nurses for the available roles will likely continue for the time being.

Nurse pay is part of the more comprehensive NHS pay system, Agenda for Change. The Agenda for Change pay structure is divided into nine bands. Each band has several points or increments, and NHS employees advance from one point to the next upon meeting specific requirements. For your first job after becoming a registered nurse, you will likely be placed in Band 5. Pay can vary by country, but at the time of publication, most newly qualified nurses can expect to be paid in the region of £28,000 – £30,000 (NHS Health Careers, 2023a). Once you have been a Band 5 nurse for over four years, you can expect pay of around £34,000 to £37,000. For comparison, the Office of National Statistics (2021) published the UK median full-time salary at £31,461 for 2020. The median wage will have increased since the figure was published, but you can see that nurses will soon earn above it as they progress through their careers.

Once you are a registered nurse, you may have the opportunity to advance in seniority according to your skills, responsibilities, and role progression. There is the potential to be promoted from Band 5 into higher bands with significant pay uplifts between each level. Nursing associates will usually be on Band 4 once qualified, with starting pay of around £25,000. Regardless of where you are on the Agenda for Change pay scale, you will also have access to the NHS Pension Scheme, considered one of the most generous and comprehensive in the UK. It provides healthcare professionals with a secure retirement income and includes benefits for dependents and provisions in case of ill-health retirement. As a registered nurse, you will also be able to explore job opportunities outside of the NHS, in private healthcare, for example, with different pay and benefits available.

Nursing is a profession that often allows individuals to have flexible work schedules. The role's responsibilities are demanding, but many employers offer work-life balance with various work options to suit different preferences and circumstances (NHS Employers, 2020). These include full-time positions, part-time positions, and opportunities for shift work. It is worth noting that the NHS and other healthcare employers provide various employment options, including zero-hours and annualised-hours contracts. These contract types offer flexibility regarding working hours and can be beneficial if you seek a more adaptable schedule. Nurses who work through agencies have the flexibility to select their preferred shifts.

Despite the potential for flexibility, nursing shift work can still impact family life, particularly if you have children/carer responsibilities. If you rely on paid childcare, shift workers are often not well accommodated, with most childcare provisions set up for Monday to Friday 8:00 am to 6:00 pm workers. A 12hr shift usually starts at 7:30 am and can finish at 8:00 pm. Allowing for travel time, this may be a problem without partner or family support available.

Activity 1.2: Reflections on a nurse's week

This reflective activity aims to help you visualise the realities of a nurse's work pattern.

Close your eyes and imagine you are working a typical week as a nurse. Consider working long shifts, perhaps twelve hours a day. Think about functioning during a weekend or night shift as part of the week's work. Visualise the atmosphere during these hours and how the change in your routine might affect you and your body's rhythm. Finally, consider how the shift pattern may impact your family and social life, possibly missing family events or social gatherings.

Question

- *After reflecting on your imagined week in the life of a nurse, identify one major challenge that stood out for you. How could you approach this challenge to maintain a balanced personal and professional life?*

A suggested answer is given at the end of the chapter.

There may also be challenges if, for example, you are a single parent and need to cover night shifts when you have minimal family support. You will be expected to work various shifts and full-time hours throughout your nursing placements. Again, worthy of consideration if you can only work part-time hours and have no cover if your child is ill. If you miss a shift during your studies, you will have to make it up as you need a minimum number of hours to qualify and register at the end of the course. Nurses are employed in rural and urban areas, with opportunities to suit most locations and circumstances. Community-based roles and clinics are often more regular hours and better suited for some. Once you have finished the nursing programme, you can seek more accommodating work that fits your needs better. For example, this might include flexibility during school holidays, although the trade-off may be working during festive holidays!

Nursing is a highly respected and valued profession that allows nurses to help people daily. It can bring a sense of purpose and job satisfaction, enabling nurses to find meaning and fulfilment in their careers. Few other professions have such a vital daily impact on people's lives. Additionally, healthcare is a field constantly changing and being shaped by emerging technology, the shifting needs of the population and evolving healthcare policies. As a nurse, you will be on the front lines of these changes, continually learning and adapting. In the next section, we will consider some challenges this can bring.

Challenges and stresses

This section will provide a direct and open discussion of the challenges and stresses of becoming a nurse. We aim to ensure you understand the downside of nursing alongside the many advantages and benefits. Nursing can be stressful, with nurses often dealing with life-and-death situations, high patient loads, and demanding work environments. Nurses may experience emotional burnout due to the intense nature of their work, which can involve caring for critically ill patients, dealing with death, and providing emotional support to patients and their families (Kumar and Jin, 2022). They can become emotionally exhausted over time, decreasing their ability to empathise and leading to feelings of detachment. This is why it is essential to cultivate coping mechanisms and self-care practices, as we will cover in Chapter 6.

Another factor to be aware of is the physical demands of being a nurse. Nurses frequently face heavy workloads, high pressure, and complex interactions. They often experience physical strain due to long hours on their feet, assisting patients, and performing other physically demanding tasks. Back pain and injuries are widespread among nurses (Duffett-Leger et al., 2022). Foot problems and other health issues can also occur. Nurses are also at a higher risk of being exposed to viruses, bacteria, and other infections due to their close contact with patients and role in invasive procedures. Despite these challenges, nurses remain resilient and dedicated, motivated by their desire to make a positive difference in the lives of their patients.

Scenario: Yasemin

Imagine you are on placement in a medical ward. You have been assisting in the care of Yasemin, a 48-year-old patient, alongside more experienced nurses. Unfortunately, you learn that she had a stroke overnight and, despite everyone's best efforts, she does not survive. As a student, it is tough. You have read about such situations, but experiencing them firsthand is an entirely different story. You wonder if there is anything else that can be done. When the senior nurse notices your concern, she speaks with you, explaining that sometimes, despite our best efforts, outcomes are beyond our control. Yasemin's family enters, and you can see the sadness in their eyes. You navigate the delicate task of supporting them, offering a listening ear and words of comfort with the help of your practice supervisor. However, there is not much time to think. The day is not over yet, and the ward is understaffed, so more work must be done. Two more patients require urgent attention. You recall your training: concentrate on the patient before you and give it your all.

Working with the team, you take charge of monitoring one of the patients reporting back to your practice supervisor when his condition deteriorates and getting involved with his emergency transfer to a high-dependency unit, which unfortunately gets delayed due to bed availability. Meanwhile, the other patient has dementia and is at high risk of falling. They require 1:1 supervision, but the ward is too understaffed to allow this. You suggest they move to a room opposite the transfer patient, enabling you and the other staff to monitor both patients safely. A suggestion that is praised for using your initiative. The minutes pass.

Sure, there are times when you feel under pressure, but there are also times when you learn and grow. As your shift ends, you have a sense of accomplishment mixed with exhaustion. It has been a long day filled with obstacles. But it has also been a day of learning: about patient care, grief, and the realities of the nursing profession.

Question

- *What strategies might you use after the shift to cope with the stress of a busy day and the death of a patient?*

A suggested answer is given at the end of the chapter.

Nurses, particularly those working in hospitals, often undertake long shifts, sometimes up to 12 hours or more. These demands can lead to fatigue and impact on work-life balance. Additionally, many nursing positions require night, weekend, and holiday shifts. It can affect your social and family life. You may have heard in the media that there has recently been strike action among nurses due to conditions and pay. The cost-of-living crisis, real-term pay cuts, patient safety concerns and high levels of nurses leaving the profession all contribute to the reasons why some nurses feel undervalued (RCN, 2022b). Nurses can face challenges such as inadequate staffing, workplace violence, and safety concerns (Kim, Mayer and Jones, 2021). These negatively impact the conditions nurses work within and partly explain why some nurses are dissatisfied and have been leaving or going on strike. It is worth noting that striking is a last resort for most healthcare professionals, as they are deeply committed to patient care and the well-being of their communities.

Understanding these challenges and stresses is not intended to discourage or persuade you but to provide a realistic picture of these aspects of being a nurse. This will help you have an informed discussion with your friends and family about your plans, as we will consider in the next section.

Speak to family and friends

It is essential to bring your family and friends into the conversation as you consider your future nursing career. These conversations can provide valuable perspectives, emotional support, and possibly even practical advice, especially if you know someone who is a nurse. Family and friends who know you well can provide insightful feedback on whether they believe you are a good fit for a nursing career. They can assist you in reflecting on your strengths, such as empathy, patience, resilience, and practical communication skills, all

Student insights

"My aunty is quite a senior nurse in a medical ward. She is so knowledgeable and I really respect her dedication. She has been giving me loads of tips and advice ... my aunty said it is a tough job, but it hasn't put me off!"

Milly, Student Nurse (Child Field)

of which are essential in nursing. They may also assist you in considering potential challenges discussed in the previous section and developing strategies to overcome them. Their advice could be particularly beneficial if any of your family members and friends are nurses. They can share first-hand experiences about the profession's rewards and challenges, talk you through the realities of the day-to-day work as a nurse, and offer advice about education and training. Even those not in the healthcare field can contribute to your decision-making process. They may raise questions or concerns you had not thought about, act as a sounding board for your ideas, and offer emotional support.

These discussions can also help prepare your loved ones for the commitment a nursing career requires. The profession can include irregular and long hours, emotional challenges, and high-stress periods. Ensuring that your family and friends understand this can aid in the development of a strong support network, which is essential for your resilience and perseverance throughout your nursing journey. Indeed, nurses often rely on their loved ones for support throughout their careers (The King's Fund, 2020). Remember that while the perspectives of others can be helpful, the final decision is yours. It should correspond to your interests, passions, and goals. Becoming a nurse is a personal journey that requires a significant commitment. However, with open conversations and the support of family and friends, it is a journey that you may not have to undertake alone.

Nursing qualifications

Several different qualifications can lead to a career in nursing. These diverse pathways provide options that accommodate different backgrounds, educational levels, and career aspirations. In this section, we will break them down and explain what is involved for each one. We start with those associated with becoming a registered nurse in one of the fields discussed earlier in the chapter, including the different university levels and qualifications. There will also be consideration of the nursing associate role.

As discussed earlier in this chapter, a registered nurse is a highly skilled healthcare professional who can provide and coordinate patient care in various settings. In the United Kingdom, becoming a registered nurse entails rigorous academic study and 2300 hours of practical training in a clinical setting (NMC, 2018b). Most nurses complete an undergraduate nursing degree, which is a three to four-year programme approved by the NMC. These programmes combine theoretical study with practical clinical placements to ensure graduates are fully prepared for the role's demands. Some students may complete a postgraduate degree to become a nurse. For an explanation of the difference between undergraduate and postgraduate study, see the concept box on the next page.

Concept box: Undergraduate vs postgraduate

An undergraduate degree, usually a bachelor's degree, is the first level of higher education a student pursues, and it typically takes three to four years to complete. It provides foundational knowledge in a specific field and various related subjects. In contrast, a postgraduate degree, such as a master's or PhD, is pursued after a person has previously graduated with a degree. It offers advanced knowledge and research opportunities in a specific area.

BSc/BSc (Hons) and BNurs undergraduate degree

A BSc in Nursing is typically a three-year full-time programme, although it may be four years for some courses in Scotland. The title of the degree may vary; examples include BSc Nursing, BSc Nursing Studies with the specific field of nursing provided after the name (e.g. BSc Nursing - Mental Health), alternatively the field may come first (e.g. BSc Mental Health Nursing). The BSc stands for Bachelor of Science, and the term 'bachelor' signifies that the degree is at the undergraduate level (see the concept box for an explanation). BNurs or BN are very similar, but the term Science is replaced with Nursing to reflect the focus of the degree more closely. Universities may offer a degree with Honours, often evident in the qualification title by the letters Hons in brackets, which involves additional study allowing you to delve deeper into your chosen field. It is worth being aware that some universities offer part-time study, although pre-registration nursing programmes are generally full-time. Applications from various academic backgrounds are accepted, but science-related experience is often recommended. See the entry requirements section in Chapter 2 for more information.

All degree programmes will include core nursing competencies such as health assessment, clinical skills, nursing theories, professional practice, and healthcare's social, political, and cultural aspects. Practical clinical experience is an integral part of each programme. As mentioned earlier in this section, you will be on placement for at least 2300 hours in healthcare settings or through simulated practice learning (NMC, 2023b). This practical experience enables you to work under the supervision of experienced healthcare professionals to apply theoretical knowledge and gain hands-on experience.

MSc and MNurs postgraduate degrees

An MSc or MNurs in a specific field of nursing is a postgraduate degree designed for people who already have a degree in another field and want to transition into nursing. It is typically a two-year accelerated programme that provides students with the knowledge and skills required to become registered nurses. The MSc abbreviation represents Master of Science, with 'master' indicating that the degree is conferred at the postgraduate level. An MSc programme combines academic study with practical and simulated clinical learning. It covers the same core proficiencies as undergraduate study but often focuses more on research, leadership, and critical thinking skills. Some MSc programmes may also provide a broader range of specialisations. You will still need to do the minimum number of hours in placement as the undergraduate routes, even though the course is often shorter. For these reasons, the MSc programme is very intensive and requires a significant time and energy commitment. However, it can be an excellent path for those who want to build upon their previous academic or professional experiences to advance their nursing career. After completing the programme in both the BSc and MSc routes, graduates can apply for registration with the NMC, which is required to practice as a Registered Nurse in the UK.

Nursing Associate

The nursing associate role is a clinical support role that is positioned between healthcare support professionals and registered nurses (NHS Health Education England, 2023). The nursing associate role was introduced a few years ago, and the training is usually delivered through an apprenticeship route. A nursing associate is an essential member of the nursing team in England who provides hands-on, person-centred care (NMC, 2023c). They are employed within healthcare, with the support to complete the training. Nursing associates make an essential contribution to nursing care but without the same level of responsibility as registered nurses, who are required to lead and manage care. This role may be suited if you want a skilled job with good variety and high levels of patient contact without the stress of being the coordinator of care. If you follow this route and are eligible, the government will pay some of your education costs. Nursing associates must complete a foundation degree which usually involves studying at a higher education level over two years (NMC, 2019). Once you start university, you will continue working while being provided with time to complete your studies and practice placements.

Activity 1.3: Registered nurse or nursing associate

This activity will help you decide if the registered nurse or nursing associate role suits your circumstances and goals. The first question you need to consider is which healthcare system you plan to work in - if the answer is not NHS England, then the nursing associate role may not be the best option for you as it is not currently a role in NHS Wales, NHS Scotland, or NHS Northern Ireland.

***Step 1**: Spend some time learning about nursing associate and registered nurse roles. Take notes on each role's qualifications, training, and career opportunities. For accurate information, the NMC website is a great place to start. Consider reading firsthand accounts of people in these roles to gain insight into their daily tasks and experiences, or view the following video which discusses the role of a nursing associate in general practice: https://bit.ly/3OuGZnE*

***Step 2**: Consider your professional goals, personal circumstances, and interests. Make notes on your long-term objectives, the amount of* *responsibility you are willing to accept, and your interest in continuing education.*

Step 3*: Examine the details you have provided for each role and consider how each relates to your responses to Step 2. This should help you determine which position best fits your career goals, personal situation, and interests.*

Questions

- *What were the most significant similarities and differences you discovered between the roles of registered nurse and nursing assistant?*
- *According to your research, which role best fits your current lifestyle, personal circumstances, and long-term goals?*

A suggested answer is given at the end of the chapter.

Nursing associates should be able to work independently and collaboratively by the end of the course, carry out and monitor care plans, and assist registered nurses in more complex procedures (NHS Health Education England, 2023). They will work alongside nurses to deliver care while freeing up the nurses' time to coordinate care and deal with any complex care needs (NMC, 2019). It is worth being aware that nursing associates can administer medication, but there may be some restrictions, and they cannot prescribe drugs. You retain employment rights while studying as a nursing associate, including your annual leave entitlement and pension. Like registered nurses, once the course is completed, all nursing associates must register with the NMC (2023c). The role provides various progression routes, and you may be able to use your nursing associate qualification to reduce the amount of studying required to become a registered nurse in future. It is a good choice if you are looking for a shorter course which enables you to earn as you learn.

Conclusion

Choosing to become a nurse is a commitment to a career full of opportunities, challenges, and the ability to have a profound impact on the lives of others. The path to nursing necessitates careful planning and a genuine commitment to lifelong professional development. Thorough research is essential for preparing for this journey. As we have explored in this chapter, it is necessary to understand the benefits of being a registered nurse while retaining awareness of the demands it can place on you. Speaking with family, friends, and professionals in the field can help paint a realistic picture of the opportunities and challenges that await. Becoming a nurse should align with your interests, strengths, and long-term career goals. While the path can be intense and complex, the rewards of making a tangible difference in people's lives provide a sense of fulfilment that few other occupations can offer. Whether you find your calling in adult, child, mental health, or learning disability nursing, each path will enable you to play an essential role in patients' healthcare journeys. In the next chapter, we will explore how to get a place on a university course, taking you a step closer to your passion.

Suggested answers

Activity 1.1

Reflecting on your personal life experiences, you may discover various elements that could lead you to a specific nursing field. For example, if you have found fulfilment assisting older adults in your family or the broader community, you may be drawn towards adult nursing. Similarly, if you have spent significant time volunteering with children or youth, this could indicate a preference for children's nursing. However, it is worth noting that such experiences do not limit you to a particular field, and your personal life experiences will likely be transferable to other fields of nursing.

Activity 1.2

One significant challenge that may have stood out for you was the potential impact of shift work on family life, especially if working on weekends or at night. These shifts can disrupt family life. It can mean missing important events like children's school events, family gatherings, and family dinners. It may require more childcare from a partner or other family members, which can strain relationships. If you are single or live alone, you may have less time to date or socialise. Shift work can also affect your mood, energy, and relationships with family and friends due to irregular sleep patterns. Fatigue or low energy may influence your off-duty time with your family. However, it is essential to remember that many nurses successfully navigate these challenges and maintain a fulfilling family and social life.

Scenario Yasemin

It can be tough when a patient dies, especially when you have formed a bond with them and their death is unexpected. You may have a lot of questions and sometimes guilt that you may have missed something that could have helped. However, it is essential to remember that certain things are out of your control. As the practice supervisor explained, people can still die despite everyone's best efforts. After a cardiac arrest or patient's death, there may be a debrief so everyone can talk about what happened, which may benefit staff morale. However, as the scenario explained, there is not always time for that. Remember to use the support networks available: speak to staff during break times, your fellow student nurses, and your practice supervisor. Keeping a journal is also a good idea to help you process your thoughts and can provide a good learning opportunity.

Activity 1.3

Several aspects may have stood out when exploring the key similarities and differences between the roles. Both registered nurses and nursing associates share a fundamental commitment to caring for patients and are essential members of any healthcare team. Both require formal education and training, and the NMC regulates their professional behaviour. However, registered nurses typically have a broader scope of practice, frequently taking on leadership roles and being involved in complex clinical decision-making. This expanded scope of practice requires a more intensive and extended degree-level education. Nursing associates, on the other hand, focus on hands-on care, undertaking clinical tasks, and supporting individuals and their families. They work with people of all ages in various healthcare settings, freeing up registered nurses to focus on more complex clinical care.

Personal reflection is required to determine which of the roles best fits your current lifestyle, personal circumstances, and long-term goals. If you are drawn to a position with a broader scope of practice and wish to undertake degree-level study, a registered nursing role may be better for you. However, a nursing assistant may be a better fit if you want to focus on providing patient care without the additional educational and practice requirements. Reflecting on which role is the best fit for you will help you identify the role that aligns with your personal and professional goals.

Recommended reading

Our Stories: 75 Years of the NHS as Told by Those Who Built, Lived, and Loved It is a publication which tells the rich history of the NHS through the eyes of ordinary people who have experienced it. It includes a heartwarming collection of stories.

The Courage of Compassion is a report by The King's Fund (2020) explores the causes and consequences of poor mental health and well-being among nurses and midwives. It provides eight key

recommendations aimed at supporting them in delivering high-quality care. You can view it here:
https://bit.ly/44aqvXq

Useful websites

Visit the ***NMC*** website to learn more about the role of the nursing associate. You can access the information here:
https://www.nmc.org.uk/about-us/our-role/who-we-regulate/nursing-associates/

The employment website '***Indeed***' has a page discussing the advantages of becoming a nurse. You can read it here:
https://www.indeed.com/career-advice/finding-a-job/advantages-of-nurse

The ***NHS Health Careers*** website provides information about the Agenda for Change pay system that covers most NHS staff, including nurses:
https://www.healthcareers.nhs.uk/working-health/working-nhs/nhs-pay-and-benefits/agenda-change-pay-rates

CHOOSING A UNIVERSITY

Introduction

Securing a place in a nursing programme at a university is a significant step toward becoming a nurse. Selecting the right university can be both exciting and intimidating. It is where you will spend several years laying the foundations for your nursing career. Choosing the right university for your circumstances and requirements is essential. It will help to consider its reputation, student facilities, teaching quality, and university culture. You will also need to think about the specifics of its nursing programme. This chapter will take you through this vital process. You will learn how to choose the right university, get insider information on what to look for and get tips on meeting the entry requirements. We will also explore other factors such as financial considerations, housing options, placements and the financial options provided to students.

So, let us start equipping you with the knowledge and clarity you need to secure your place.

Universities and nursing courses

The university you attend will substantially impact your academic experience and future career opportunities. There are several things to consider when exploring your options, including the campus environment, culture, and local job opportunities. Learning more about the reputation of each nursing course and university is helpful before deciding where to study. A useful starting point in your research is to consult one or more university league tables. These rank universities based on factors such as overall performance, subject-specific rankings, student satisfaction, and graduate prospects. We will now introduce a few popular league tables.

One league table to consider is the Complete University Guide (2023a). This guide ranks the best universities in the UK and provides a breakdown for 74 subject areas. It allows you to narrow the rankings by region, entry requirements, student satisfaction, and graduate prospects. Another league table to consider is the Guardian (2023) University Guide which ranks UK universities by subject, student satisfaction, staff numbers, spending, and career opportunities. The Times Higher Education (2023) World University Rankings feature universities worldwide, emphasising research, teaching, knowledge transfer, and global outlook. Another option is the QS World University Rankings (2023), which again ranks universities and lets you contrast institutions based on various criteria, including academic reputation and the number of international students enrolled. We have included links to all these league tables within the useful websites section at the end of the chapter.

As well as the overall league position of the university, it is also very worthwhile looking at their rankings for nursing. Activity 2.1 will help you make a start with this.

Activity 2.1: Online research

In this activity, you will use UK university league tables to compare three universities that may be options for you to study nursing. By completing this activity, you will better understand the nursing programmes offered by various universities and decide which university might be the best fit for you. You will use the following databases for this activity:

- ***Complete University Guide's Nursing Rankings*** *https://bit.ly/3DUbcaX*
- ***The Guardian's Nursing and Midwifery League Table*** *https://bit.ly/3QHYd3B*

Start by choosing three universities that interest you. On a piece of paper or computer, create a comparison table with the following columns: University Name, Ranking for Nursing (Complete University Guide), Ranking for Nursing (The Guardian) and any other factors you find essential. Search the database for each university and use the information you find to fill in the relevant columns in the table. Finally, compare the universities based on the information in your table and consider using it as part of your decision-making process.

Question

- *Why might the highest-ranked university not be the best option for you?*

A suggested answer is given at the end of the chapter.

Attending university open days or virtual events may be beneficial to gain insight into the course and institution. It will enable you to visit the facilities and talk to staff in person, allowing you to see beyond the glossy brochures. Look for nursing schools with modern and well-equipped facilities. Look at the nursing facilities such as simulated wards; do they seem well equipped and set up for different clinical and community scenarios? An insider tip: ask how the facilities are used during the first year to support student learning. The answer will give you an idea of how much you will use them during your studies.

If you are interested in a specific field of nursing, check that the university offers specialisations in those areas. Is this reflected in the facilities available? Do they have a simulated paediatric ward if you are interested in children's nursing, for example? Write down some questions to ask about the learning and teaching approaches used to see if they suit your learning style. Consider the variety and quality of placement opportunities, as these can influence your learning and future career prospects. Also, investigate the likelihood of a job once you qualify. A larger town or city may offer various experiences across different fields of nursing, whereas these may be more limited in a rural setting. Try to get a feel for the course. Do the staff seem approachable, knowledgeable, and friendly? Finally, ask how nursing students are supported with their studies and listen carefully to the response. It will provide insight into what to expect while on the course.

Location, facilities, and culture

One of the main things to consider is the location of the university. Would you rather live on campus in a university residence hall or find your housing off campus? Examine the price, location, and quality of student housing offered by the university and the surrounding area. Consider your housing options carefully; limited university and rental accommodation may be available in some regions. Check the cost and availability near the university. Perhaps you already have a house or will live at home with your parents. This setup may be advantageous from a financial perspective, and a positive home environment can assist with stressors that may arise during the nursing programme (Hall and Zygmunt, 2021). However, living at home can influence your sense of belonging at university as there may be fewer opportunities to develop social relationships than other living arrangements such as university halls of residence (Pokorny, Holley and Kane, 2017). Both situations have pros and cons, so think carefully about what is best for you.

If you choose to live away from the university, ensuring easy access to the campus and placement areas is essential. Is public transport available, and how much will this cost each month? Can you access discounted or free travel, as is the case in Scotland if you are under 22 and meet the eligibility criteria? Alternatively, is affordable parking available nearby - remember that you will be on campus regularly during your nursing studies. The Open University (2023) is worth consideration if you already work in healthcare, as it may allow you to stay in your job while you study. With its online presence, your location can be more flexible. You will still need to think about your ability to attend placements across the local area. Some universities have placement areas across a large geographical area, particularly those outside large towns and cities. These factors may influence your choices, especially if you do not drive or need to factor in childcare costs for longer travel times or having to stay overnight.

Activity 2.2: Making an informed decision

This activity will assist you in identifying and prioritising your options when selecting a university. The focus is on location, facilities, and culture, although you can add other areas as desired. It should help you make a more informed and personalised decision when choosing a place to study.

Step 1: *Take a few moments to consider what you want out of your university experience. Focus on location, facilities, and culture and write* *down whatever comes to mind.*

Step 2: *Next, make three columns on a sheet of paper with the headings 'location', 'facilities', and 'culture'. List the factors that are important to you under each heading. For instance, under 'location' include aspects such as proximity to family, the appeal of the city or town, access to healthcare facilities, cost of living, and availability of accommodation. Under 'facilities', you can include areas such as the library, lab facilities and equipment, recreational facilities, and so on. When listing under 'culture', you might wish to consider factors such as student body and staff diversity, inclusivity, support services, and student-led organisations on campus.*

Step 3: *Once you have your lists, rank the items in each category from least to most important. Viewing the results will assist you in visualising which factors are most critical in your decision-making process as you explore which university to attend.*

Question

- *How did your perception of your priorities change, if at all, after completing this activity? Were there any unexpected results?*

A suggested answer is given at the end of the chapter.

A university's physical layout and facilities can significantly impact your student experience. Amenities include libraries, study spaces, sports facilities, and student unions. You may be able to get a tour of the university during open days, so take a good look around. Find out about the support systems such as academic guidance, personal tutoring, and mental health services. If you have additional support needs, looking for the support available at the place you wish to study is vital. We have provided some further details about these factors within Chapter 6. You can also get a sense of the culture during a visit. Culture is a broad concept that includes the values, norms, and social life that define the student experience. It is associated with forming a student identity through participation within the learning culture (Mallman and Lee, 2017). Some universities may have a lively social scene emphasising student organisations and events, whereas others may have a quieter, more academic-focused atmosphere. If you get the opportunity to speak with current students, take it. They can often give you a low-down on what it is like to study at the university and will be able to answer questions that you may not want to ask the staff! Consider your environment and look for a university that matches your preferences.

Entry requirements

Meeting the entry requirements for the nursing programme is critical in securing a place at the university. The requirements vary depending on the university and the nursing programme you are applying to. They generally include academic qualifications, health and character checks, and sometimes group/individual interviews or entrance tests. Academic qualifications typically include a set number of UCAS points earned from A-levels, Highers, or equivalent qualifications, with at least one subject related to health or science. Science subjects may include psychology or sociology. There will often be specific requirements for English and maths.

Vocational qualifications such as BTEC, NVQ, HNC, HND and SVQ may also help you to meet the entry requirements. Some universities may have an arrangement where you can apply to join the second year of a nursing programme if you have completed a vocational qualification, such as the HNC Healthcare Practice available in Scotland. Ask the admissions team at the university for advice about whether you meet the entry requirements.

Student insights

"I didn't have the entry requirements for my course ... so I went to college at night to do the qualifications. It took me longer to get in, but I felt more prepared when I started at uni."

Craig, Student Nurse (Mental Health Field)

For nursing associate training, you will need English and maths at GCSEs grades 9 to 4 (A to C) or Functional Skills Level 2 (NHS Health Careers, 2023b). Some employers may also ask for a level 3 qualification, and you will need to show that you can study for a foundation degree level and complete the Nursing Associate Apprenticeship programme.

Please do not be too disheartened if you do not meet the entry requirements. Find out what you need to complete and explore ways to achieve them. Many nursing students have completed a qualification through night classes at college to meet the requirements. Some universities may have an access or foundation course designed to prepare you for a nursing degree, and the credits may count towards the entry – ask the university what is available. If you applied through UCAS and have not received any offers or did not meet the conditions of your offers, you can apply for a course via clearing. Clearing is a service operated by UCAS (2023a) that helps universities fill any spaces left for the upcoming year, sometimes including their nursing programmes. Check the useful websites at the chapter's end to learn more about this process.

You should check for necessary English language qualifications if you are an international applicant. There will also be immigration requirements to consider, and the university can advise you about the process. Whatever your situation, try to begin the application process as early as possible. Starting well before the deadline will enable you to manage any issues, ensure you have more university options, and prevent you from rushing through your choices.

Personal Statement

You will usually be required to write a personal statement as part of your UCAS (2023b) application. It provides a chance to explain why you are interested in nursing and why you would be a good fit for the programme and the profession. The personal statement is limited to 4,000 characters and allows you to show how your values and attributes align with nursing. The introduction to your personal statement should be captivating and help the admissions tutor get to know you (UCAS, 2023b). It might include a personal anecdote or a powerful declaration of your passion for nursing. The goal is to get the reader's interest immediately and demonstrate your commitment to a future in the profession. In the main body of your personal statement, you should emphasise your knowledge and understanding. It would be helpful to describe what you believe the role entails, the challenges it may present, and the fulfilment it may provide.

Discuss any work placements, volunteering, or relevant experiences you have had in healthcare settings. Most hospitals have a volunteer programme, and it may be beneficial to consider this before or during the application process. Although you will not provide direct care, it will offer insights into the healthcare setting and provide opportunities to speak to people working there. Seeing the nursing role first-hand can be a game changer – either cementing in your mind that it is for you or leading you to consider another healthcare profession. Likewise, personal experience in providing informal care is also relevant. Suppose you have been involved with looking after a family member with a long-term health condition. This type of care experience is suitable for inclusion within your personal statement.

Activity 2.3: Familiarisation with the personal statement

UCAS has personal statement advice for nursing available on their website: https://bit.ly/3YwpN5X

Visit this site to learn how to construct a personal statement. It includes suggestions for structuring the statement, demonstrating your understanding of the role and field you are applying for, and reflecting on your skills, attributes, and values. A key recommendation from UCAS is that you write about how you arrived at your decision to go into nursing.

Question

- *What are the key reasons why you have decided to become a nurse? Write a paragraph setting these out and include specific information about why you chose a particular field of nursing.*

A suggested answer is given at the end of the chapter.

UCAS (2023c) has provided a Personal Statement Worksheet that you may find helpful: https://bit.ly/44bhj5o

The worksheet may help you structure the statement and include relevant information. A compelling personal statement will highlight your unique skills and qualities. For example, you could demonstrate your ability in teamwork, problem-solving, empathy, or resilience. Draw upon specific examples from your academic, professional, or personal life, providing a real-world example to demonstrate the application of your skills and knowledge (UCAS, 2023d. Academic achievements that have prepared you for a nursing degree should be highlighted. Perhaps you studied biology or psychology, enabling you to show how they relate to nursing. Finish your personal statement by summarising why you want to study nursing and how it fits with your long-term goals. Aim to leave the reader with a lasting, positive impression. Remember to carefully proofread your statement for spelling, grammar, and punctuation errors before submission.

Applicant interview and screening

Not so long ago, most universities required applicants to undertake an individual interview in person. Over recent years many universities have replaced these with alternative approaches. These may include values-based activities, written exercises, group discussions, and online interviews. Regardless of the process, the critical thing to remember is that the university is checking that you have thought about your choice to study nursing and display the appropriate attributes. You should aim to learn about the specific course you have applied for and the standards that nurses need to meet. The NMC (2018a) Code of Professional Standards is a great starting point. A mistake that many applicants make during the interview process is to display a lack of understanding of what the nursing role entails. You may already work in healthcare, and if so, do not be afraid to share your experiences during the application process. As discussed in the previous section, volunteering or seeking healthcare employment can be worthwhile to provide direct experience.

Applicants may also share personal healthcare experiences, reflecting upon their own experiences of receiving care or those related to looking after a family member. You should only share things that you feel comfortable sharing and always try to demonstrate a broader grasp of the nursing role when describing personal experiences. If you do not have any related experiences, this should not prevent you from showing relevant understanding through other forms of research. Discussions with a family member or friend familiar with nursing can pay off. If you do not have anyone to speak to, try going online to find out about the day in the life of a nurse. The RCN (2021) has a fascinating and inspiring page titled *Day in the Life of a Newly Registered Nurse* on their website. It will provide valuable insights that can help you be more informed, and the full address is available in the useful websites section at the end of the chapter.

Scenario: Abdul and Adam

An essential part of becoming a nurse is success during the application process. Adam and Abdul, two applicants for a Mental Health Nursing programme, respond differently to questions about the profession. Both candidates have valid mental health nursing perspectives, but their approaches differ. Read the scenario below and then answer the questions that follow.

During the application process, Adam made a point of emphasising his caring personality. Adam feels he is a very kind person and has helped family members when they have been going through difficulties. When asked about the role of the mental health nurse, he explains that they care after others until they feel well again. On the other hand, Abdul discussed the profession's nuances when asked similar questions. Abdul discusses the need for empathy and trust when developing a therapeutic relationship with individuals experiencing a mental health crisis. He provided brief definitions of these concepts and how they align with his values. Abdul explained how a mental health nurse must demonstrate compassion while using evidence-based interventions to help clients recover.

Questions

- *Why is Adam or Abdul more likely to succeed in applying for the Mental Health Nursing programme?*
- *What approaches might you use to gain knowledge that will assist during the application process?*

A suggested answer is given at the end of the chapter.

Try to have a clear idea of the field of nursing you wish to study before the interview process. It comes across well if you provide a clear rationale for studying adult nursing rather than saying you do not mind which nursing field you will pursue. It can be worth researching interview techniques, and there are lots of video guides on platforms such as YouTube. Write down possible questions that may come up and then practise how you would answer them. It can be helpful to ask family or friends to help you prepare by asking the questions and providing feedback on your answers. The university staff may be interested in why you chose their university, so look online at its history and the strengths of its nursing programme. You may also refer to the league table rankings discussed earlier in this chapter.

Because nursing work is physically and mentally demanding, applicants must undergo health checks to ensure they are fit for practice. It usually entails filling out a health questionnaire, and you may experience a medical screening through an occupational health service. It is essential to disclose any health issues you have during this process as it is designed to ensure you are fit to undertake the role (NHS Employers, 2021). The university can then consider your health during the admissions process and put support in place as required. Due to close contact with vulnerable individuals, all nursing students must also complete a disclosure check. These are called Disclosure and Barring Service (DBS) checks in England and Wales (UK Government, 2023a). Disclosure Scotland carries out the equivalent checks in Scotland (Scottish Government, 2023), while in Northern Ireland, they are handled by Access NI (NI Direct, 2023a). The check involves filling out a form and sending it to the service. They then check for criminal records and review information held by the police and other agencies as necessary. The university will receive a copy of the report, and it is a way for the university to verify there is nothing that would present a risk in the context of your role as a student nurse.

Conclusion

Selecting the right university is a multifaceted decision that requires research and careful consideration of numerous factors. When choosing a programme like nursing, which requires features academic and practical components, the decision becomes even more complicated. During this chapter, we started by comparing nursing courses based on their league table ranking and other factors. We also consider how the university's location, facilities, and culture significantly impact the student experience. Considering entry requirements will help you choose a programme that matches your academic qualifications and skills. At the same time, we have learnt about the interview and screening processes. Understanding these factors will help you confidently proceed through the application process. The next chapter will explore what you should do once you have secured a place.

Suggested answers

Activity 2.1

While rankings can be an excellent place to start when researching university courses, they may not be the best fit for every student nurse applicant. They frequently consider a wide range of factors that may not be directly related to the quality of education and experience a student nurse receives. The ranking of the nursing programme will only be one factor in your decision, complete activity 2.2 to establish other priorities that may be relevant. You could even combine the tables to help you with a more comprehensive overview of each activity. Writing down and comparing the information in your table will help you to organise your decision-making.

Activity 2.2

You may have discovered that writing down your priorities helped you identify the aspects of your university experience that are most important to you. We often have preconceived notions about what should be prioritised regarding factors such as facilities or location. However, through reflection and prioritisation, you may have discovered that the university's culture is important to you – including the sense of community and available support services. If so, this may have surprised you because it contradicted your initial thoughts. This realisation can significantly impact your decision-making process, personalising it and ensuring that your chosen university will meet your specific needs and expectations.

Activity 2.3

This activity may have helped you understand why you chose nursing as the career you wish to pursue. You would likely have thought about personal or work-related experiences that have drawn you towards a specific field of nursing. It may have brought to the surface values or attributes aligned with your nursing field. You may think about your desire for personal and professional growth and how this is necessary for becoming a nurse.

Scenario: Abdul and Adam

Based on their application process and responses, Abdul appears to have a better chance of being accepted into the Mental Health Nursing programme. Although both candidates exhibit important qualities, Abdul demonstrates a deeper understanding of the role's complexities and requirements. His ability to discuss empathy and trust, as well as his knowledge of evidence-based interventions, all indicate that he has a more comprehensive understanding of the role of a mental health nurse. This knowledge should help position him for success during the application process.

You can improve your application and understanding of nursing by using several methods. If you do not have any healthcare experience, you can look into volunteering in a health and social care setting. Working with diverse patient populations will help you understand the role of health and social care professionals, develop essential nursing characteristics, and understand how interdisciplinary teams work. We have provided recommended reading and useful websites at the end of each chapter that may help you prepare for applying. Networking with nursing students or professionals can provide insights and advice about the profession and application process.

Recommended reading

How to Complete your UCAS Application – 2024 Entry by Duncan Chamberlain (2023) is written in association with UCAS. It provides practical step-by-step guidance on the application process.

Useful websites

Complete University Guide contains information about the league tables which rank universities on a national, regional, and subject-area basis. It also provides clearing advice and offers a personalised tool to help you find the best course.
https://www.thecompleteuniversityguide.co.uk/

Guardian University Guide provides a guide to the best UK universities based on factors such as student satisfaction, staff numbers, spending, and career opportunities. It enables you to search for a course by subject area, region, or institution and compare university rankings.
https://www.theguardian.com/education/universityguide

NHS Health Careers provides information on entry requirements for nursing, alternative qualifications, and details about financial support while studying at university.

https://www.healthcareers.nhs.uk/explore-roles/nursing/

QS World University Rankings covers topics such as the best universities, business schools, and student cities in the world, as well as the most recent news and advice for prospective students.

https://www.topuniversities.com/university-rankings

The ***RCN*** has several resources which provide insights into the nursing role. You can visit it to find out more about the day in the life of a newly registered nurse.

https://www.rcn.org.uk/Get-Involved/Forums/NRN-network/Day-in-the-life-of-a-newly-registered-nurse

Times Higher Education World University Rankings offers an overview of the rankings for 1,799 universities in 104 countries and regions based on 13 performance indicators. It also includes highlights from the ranking results, such as the top universities.

https://www.timeshighereducation.com/world-university-rankings/2023/world-ranking

UCAS provides information about clearing and what to do on results day.

https://www.ucas.com/undergraduate/clearing-and-results-day/what-clearing

WHAT TO DO BEFORE YOU START

Introduction

As you take a deep breath and count down to the first day of your studies, there are a few things you can do to prepare. This chapter will guide you through the process of getting ready for induction and beyond. It starts with a detailed exploration of the different funding options available. These are complex and can vary between the nations, so we have broken down what is available in each country. The chapter will also introduce you to reading and equipment worth considering as you prepare to begin your studies. These details will help you identify reliable information sources and learn about the equipment you will encounter during the early stages of your studies. The chapter concludes with a section on the NMC standards and how they influence nursing education and practice. The content should help you feel more confident about starting the course, remembering that preparation today will pave the way for success tomorrow.

Funding your studies

The financial arrangements that are available to study nursing can be complex. You will need to explore your options before you start your programme, and it is generally advisable to apply for funding as early as possible. This section will explain the primary funding sources and discuss how they apply to nursing students. The funding system differs between England, Wales, Scotland, and Northern Ireland, so we have broken down the sections to enable you to read the relevant part. Funding criteria are regularly updated and may vary depending on your circumstances, so we have provided links to further details. Many nursing students undertake paid work to help supplement other income while completing the nursing programme. We will discuss the pros and cons of working alongside your studies in the next chapter. However, it is worth mentioning that if you plan to work as a healthcare support worker to help fund your studies, applying a few months before you start at university would be worthwhile. Some hospitals only take on bank staff twice a year, and the process can take at least six weeks due to disclosure clearances and health checks.

Loans

A student loan is money borrowed to help pay for university. You are most likely to require a student loan if you live in England, as other nations have different funding arrangements for most nursing students. A student loan is intended to assist students in paying for their education and associated costs such as tuition, books and supplies, and living expenses. The Student Loans Company (2023) provides funding which you can check if you are eligible and apply online via the UK Government: *https://bit.ly/3QybP1o*

The maintenance loan is used for living costs, and the amount you can receive is linked to your age and whether you live with your parents. The loan is paid directly into your bank account at the start of each term. Repayment terms vary depending on the loan but generally begin after completing the course and earning above a certain income level (UK Government, 2023b). While student loans can help pay for a nursing degree, it is essential to understand the long-term commitment involved.

Activity 3.1: Funding research

If you are from England or the European Union, you may find the student finance calculator helpful: https://bit.ly/45stsnv

Use it to receive an estimate for the student loan amount you can expect and any additional student funding available. There are several pieces of information you need to input, regarding your circumstances, such as where you will live while studying. Once completed, you will receive an indication of how much maintenance loan you can apply for and information about tuition fees.

Questions

Once you have carried out the calculation, answer the following:

- *What is the maximum Maintenance Loan available?*
- *How much are you eligible for? We recommend that you note this figure and then complete activity 3.2.*

A suggested answer is given at the end of the chapter.

Tuition Fees

Tuition Fees are the costs associated with attending university. They cover the costs of your classes and instruction. The amount varies depending on where you study, your course, and whether you are a UK, EU, or international student. Due to the devolution of educational powers, the tuition fee system in the United Kingdom varies significantly between England, Wales, Scotland, and Northern Ireland. See the relevant section below for further information.

England

At the time of writing, undergraduate students from England can be charged up to £9,250 per year for a full-time degree (UK Government, 2023c). As discussed in the previous section, the Student Loans Company (2023) provides loans and grants to eligible students, which can be used to pay tuition fees. Nursing students will repay the loan plus interest. As a nursing student, you may also qualify for the NHS Learning Support Fund, which is discussed later in this chapter.

Wales

Nursing students in Wales may be able to access the NHS Wales Bursary Scheme, which covers the cost of tuition fees and provides additional financial support. More details about the scheme and eligibility are provided in the bursary section of this chapter. You can also find further information here:
https://bit.ly/47vnhAU

Scotland

Most nursing students studying in Scotland do not have to pay tuition fees. The Student Awards Agency Scotland (SAAS) will pay your tuition if you normally live in Scotland. There are specific residency requirements in place that you may need to check. It is worth being aware that if you are from another part of the UK studying in Scotland, you will usually get charged tuition fees. More details about the scheme and eligibility are provided in the bursary section of this chapter. You can also find further information here:
https://bit.ly/3Yxus7C

Northern Ireland

Nursing students from Northern Ireland have different funding arrangements than most other higher education students. You will

not need to pay tuition fees, although there are residency requirements. More details about the scheme and eligibility are provided in the bursary section of this chapter. You can also find further information here:
https://bit.ly/47xgsyz

Postgraduate tuition fees

Postgraduate tuition fees vary, but you may still be able to apply for a loan. Your employer may also be able to offer support. Postgraduate study (e.g. MSc Nursing) often has different funding arrangements. Find out more from the UK Government here:
https://www.gov.uk/funding-for-postgraduate-study
There is also information available from UCAS:
https://www.ucas.com/postgraduate/postgraduate-fees-and-funding

Scenario: Aishah

Aishah is currently finishing her A-levels and is interested in pursuing a career in nursing. Because she lives in Bristol, her first thought was to attend a university within travelling distance from the family home. However, she is also drawn toward studying away from home in Wales or Scotland to broaden her experiences and perspectives. Aishah begins her research into the various universities in England, Wales, and Scotland. She discovers that each university has its distinct advantages. An essential factor she considers is the financial impact of studying in these various countries. She knows staying home would save her money on rent and living expenses in Bristol. However, the financial support available in other countries may assist with her living expenses if she meets the eligibility criteria. Aishah learns that Scotland and Wales have different funding support for student nurses when compared to England. For Aishah, aside from money, there are a range of other factors to consider. She wonders how the differences in nursing curriculum and career opportunities in the different areas will affect her future career. She contrasts the ease of being in her familiar living environment with the excitement of moving to a new place. To make a more informed decision about her future, she makes notes of the advantages and disadvantages of studying close to home or further afield.

Question

- *Given her financial situation, how might Aishah compare the financial benefits of studying close to home in Bristol versus further afield in Wales or Scotland?*

A suggested answer is given at the end of the chapter.

NHS Learning Support Fund (LSF)

If you are studying nursing at a university in England, you may be eligible to apply to the NHS Learning Support Fund. Applicants must be eligible for tuition fees and maintenance loan support from the Student Loans Company (SLC) (NHS Business Services Authority, 2022). There are other inclusion and exclusion criteria, and you can find out more here: *https://bit.ly/45sUACJ*

At the time of writing, you can receive the following:

- A training grant of £5,000 per academic year.
- Parental support of £2,000, if you have at least one dependent child under 15 years or under 17 years if registered with special educational needs.
- Money back for excess travel and temporary accommodation costs (Travel and Dual Accommodation Expenses) while you are on your practice placement.
- Support for students experiencing financial hardship (Exceptional Support Fund).

(NHS Business Services Authority, 2022, p.1)

You can start your application from the 1st of March when starting your studies in September or October of the same year. The payments are made in three instalments across the academic year.

Bursary

A bursary is funding provided to assist you in paying for your education or other costs such as books or travel. Unlike a student loan, a bursary does not need to be paid back. The nursing bursary system differs between England, Wales, Scotland, and Northern Ireland. Please keep in mind that arrangements are subject to residency, course type, and personal circumstances, so please check for up-to-date information with the relevant funding bodies in each country.

England

The nursing bursary, which used to cover tuition fees and provide a maintenance grant in England, was abolished in 2017. However, as discussed earlier in this section, you may be eligible for the NHS Learning Support Fund.

Wales

Students studying pre-registration nursing in Wales may be eligible to apply for NHS Wales Bursary Scheme (Health Education and Improvement Wales, 2022): *https://bit.ly/47vnhAU*

To receive the bursary, you must agree to work in Wales for two years after finishing the programme (or 18 months for certain accelerated programmes) and meet the terms and conditions of the scheme. It covers tuition fees, a means-tested bursary for living expenses, a £1,000 non-means-tested grant, and assistance with travel, placement accommodation and childcare. If eligible, you may also have access to a reduced student loan.

Scotland

In Scotland, nursing students can apply for a Scottish Government bursary, which includes a non-repayable bursary for living expenses and a supplementary grant for additional costs such as travel or dependent's allowance. At the time of writing, the bursary is worth

£10,000 a year, paid monthly throughout the course. There is also a discretionary fund for those who are having financial difficulties. Residency conditions apply, so check the details on the Scottish Government (2022) website and search for paramedic, nursing, and midwifery student support: *https://bit.ly/3OWxGhK*

You can also find out more about the funding available via the Student Awards Agency Scotland: *https://bit.ly/4499tZS*

Northern Ireland

If you are from Northern Ireland, you can apply for a bursary to cover tuition fees and help with living expenses (NI Direct, 2023b). You will need to have lived in Northern Ireland for the last three years to qualify for the bursary. The amount of the bursary is determined by individual and family income, with potential additional allowances for special circumstances such as disability or dependents. Find out more here: *https://bit.ly/47xgsyz*

Scholarships

Scholarships are similar to bursaries in that money is provided to you to help pay for your education, and you usually do not have to pay back. Nursing scholarships may be given out by universities, healthcare organisations, non-profit organisations, or even government agencies. The eligibility requirements for these scholarships can vary greatly (UCAS, 2023e). In terms of nurse education, there are different types of scholarships, including those aimed towards international students, undergraduate students from other parts of the UK, and post-graduate nursing students. You will need to undertake some online research to find out what may be available for your specific circumstances.

Activity 3.2: Financial health check

Undertaking a financial health check is a simple yet effective way to evaluate your current financial situation and ensure that you are on the right path to meet your financial goals. It is essential to understand the impact of studying nursing on your finances. You can complete the financial health check in advance of starting the course or while studying. This short activity will help you create a realistic budget by assessing your income and expenses. Tracking your spending and finding ways to save should help match your financial priorities to the available income.

Step 1: *List or estimate all the income sources and the monthly amount received as a student nurse. Include any student loans, bursaries, or scholarships that you are eligible for. Income from part-time work, financial aid or family contributions and any other income sources should also be included.*

Step 2: *Keep track of your expenses for a month. This should include all your bills, groceries, transportation, educational supplies, entertainment, eating out, and unanticipated costs. If you have not started university yet, use the projected expenses you expect to spend while studying. Try using a notebook or budgeting app on your phone to make this easier.*

Step 3: *Categorise your expenses: Divide your costs into 'needs' (rent, bills, groceries, etc.) and 'wants; (entertainment, eating out). This will help* *you track where your money is going and identify your priorities.*

Step 4: *Make a budget: Make a budget based on your income and expenses. Have a set amount of money for each category and stick to it while studying.*

Step 5: *Review and adjust: Frequently review your spending and compare it to your budget. Make any necessary adjustments, and remember that your budget may need to change as your situation changes.*

Question

- *How might completing this activity assist with progressing effectively during your studies?*

A suggested answer is given at the end of the chapter.

Hardship funding

Hardship funding, also known as an emergency fund, is assistance that is made available for students facing financial difficulties. It is money that universities may be able to provide if you are in hardship due to your current circumstances (UK Government, 2023d). This money is intended to provide short-term support, and you are usually not required to repay it. These difficulties can result from various factors, including unexpected loss of your job or home, medical emergencies, or delays in other funding sources. Hardship funds are frequently limited and intended to be students' last resort. You may also be able to apply to other organisations, such as the RCN Foundation (2023), in certain circumstances. The eligibility criteria and application process for hardship funding differ from institution to institution. There may be some information on the university website, but it is often worth speaking with an advisor from student services to find more information.

> ***Student insights***
>
> *"I was really struggling with my uni work as I was doing it all on my phone as my laptop had broken and it was too much to buy a new one. My tutor said I should speak with the people at the student hub to see what help I could get. They gave me money for a laptop and it helped a lot."*
>
> *Bernadette, Student Nurse (Learning Disability Field)*

Universal Credit

If you are eligible for Universal Credit (UK Government, 2023e), knowing how your entitlement may be affected when you become a nursing student is essential. There can also be implications for other benefits, such as the Personal Independence Payment or Carer's Allowance. The eligibility for Universal Credit and other benefits when studying as a nurse in the UK can vary across England, Scotland, Wales, and Northern Ireland. Remember that policies and regulations can change over time, so it is always best to check with local authorities or official government websites for the most up-to-date information. Student nurses are generally considered full-time students for benefit purposes. You may not be eligible for Universal Credit unless you fall into a specific category, such as being a parent, having a disability, or being part of a couple where the partner qualifies. If you fall into one of these categories, receipt of a student loan or other income may or may not be considered when calculating your entitlement. This fact is one of the reasons why the calculation can become quite complex, so it is best to seek professional advice from a local welfare advisor or student support service. You may also consider contacting relevant government agencies who can provide detailed information tailored to individual circumstances. Additionally, the RCN provides a guide explaining how Universal Credit may be influenced by student income: *https://bit.ly/3ODv07q*

Reading and research

One of the best ways to prepare for your nursing career is to engage in some insightful reading. While you are not expected to have extensive nursing knowledge before beginning your course, reading up on a few key concepts can make the initial transition into nursing education a little easier. This book has been specifically designed to help you achieve this, but other types of resources can also be helpful. Textbooks included in the programme can serve as a good starting point, and you may be provided with a suggested reading list during your admission process. Nursing textbooks that cover fundamental concepts may be useful at this stage, and we have provided some examples at the end of this chapter. Reading articles from reputable nursing journals can provide you with an understanding of current issues and clinical guidance. There is often a charge to read academic papers, whereas you will usually get free access through your university once enrolled. It can be worth scanning nursing journals' free content, but we would not recommend buying access at this stage. Here are some examples to consider:

- Nursing Standard: *https://rcni.com/nursing-standard*
- Nursing Times: *https://www.nursingtimes.net/*
- BJN: *https://info.britishjournalofnursing.com/*

Reading about personal experiences can give you a realistic view of nursing. For example, 'The Language of Kindness: A Nurse's Story,' by Christie Watson, provides an intimate look into the profession. If you decide to buy any books for your studies, you may be able to receive a student discount (see the concept box).

Many students sell their books when they finish the course, so you can get discounted texts on bookseller sites that are relatively up-to-date. Sometimes family members or friends might ask if there are any books they can buy as a gift to help get you started with your studies, so consider the ones in the recommended reading section if you are lucky enough to have this opportunity. While not compulsory, pre-course reading will familiarise you with the language and context of nursing, making the transition to becoming a student nurse easier.

Concept box: Student discounts

Many booksellers, including online and high street shops, will offer a student discount once you are enrolled. Receiving these discounts requires you to register as a student and submit evidence of your status when buying online. You may be asked to show your student ID at the time of purchase if shopping in the high street. Your university will be able to provide proof of your enrolment on the course, and often you access this by logging into your personal student record and searching for a letter confirming your status. Ask student services for assistance if you cannot find the required evidence. There are also apps and services you can sign up for. These companies also verify your student status and then provide discounts for purchases with different companies. They provide opportunities to buy books and many other things at a discount, and Student Beans and UNiDAYS are two popular examples. Find out more via the following:

- *Student Beans: https://www.studentbeans.com/uk*
- *UNiDAYS: https://www.myunidays.com/GB/en-GB*

Equipment

During your nursing education, you will become familiar with clinical equipment. In this section, we have identified items you will commonly encounter during the early stages of your studies. It is worth being aware of the equipment listed below, but remember that you will learn how to use them effectively and safely during your studies. You do not usually require to purchase any of these items as they will be available during skills classes or placement, although many student nurses invest in a fob watch.

Stethoscope: This essential tool enables you to listen to the sounds of the heart, lungs, and other organs. It can be used to assess patients and track changes in their condition.

Sphygmomanometer: A blood pressure cuff is a device that measures a patient's blood pressure. You will likely become familiar with both manual and electronic sphygmomanometers.

Thermometer: A thermometer is a device used to measure the body's temperature. There are several types of thermometers that you will encounter during your studies, including oral, ear, and forehead strips, and in some settings, rectal thermometers.

Pulse Oximeter: A pulse oximeter is a small device that clips onto a patient's finger or earlobe to measure the oxygen saturation in their blood. It can help inform the respiratory assessment.

Penlight: Nurses use penlights to check pupils' responsiveness and examine patients' mouths and throats.

Fob watch: Many nursing tasks require accurate timing, such as taking a patient's pulse or respiratory rate. A fob watch can often be worn on your uniform to help with patient assessment but check local policies. If you are considering getting a fob watch, choose one that will not harbour bacteria. A silicone fob watch with a removable face can be thoroughly cleaned, making it suitable from an infection control perspective.

Activity 3.3: Nursing apps

Review the following healthcare-related apps to discover their offering and help decide if they may be useful during your studies. You should be able to search for them online or view options in the app store on your phone or other device.

- *BMJ Best Practice app.*
- *BNF Publications app.*
- *British Red Cross First Aid app.*
- *NHS app.*

Question

- *Write a short summary for each app and decide which ones may be worth using during your studies.*

A suggested answer is given at the end of the chapter.

You will also want to consider non-clinical equipment that will be useful for your studies. Aside from items such as notepads and pens, it is worth investing in a laptop or computer with word-processing software if you can afford it. This will help you study and complete assessments without being dependent on university computers. As discussed earlier in this chapter, some universities will help with the cost of IT equipment, particularly for students in hardship. Speak with Student Services to see if any assistance is available.

Nursing and Midwifery Council

The NMC plays an essential role in the nursing profession, so becoming acquainted with this organisation is a helpful step before beginning your studies. As mentioned in the first chapter, the NMC (2022a) is the UK's independent regulator for the nursing and midwifery professions. It was established in 2002 to replace the United Kingdom Central Council for Nursing, Midwifery, and Health Visiting (UKCC). The organisation has been tasked with raising professional standards and modernising the regulatory framework. The NMC is based in London and serves the entire United Kingdom. Its overarching responsibility is to protect the public by establishing standards of education, training, conduct, and performance for nurses and midwives to adhere to. The NMC (2018a) publishes the Code of Conduct, which outlines the professional standards nurses, midwives, and nursing associates must uphold. Familiarising yourself with the Code will provide you with an understanding of the ethical and professional standards you will be expected to maintain throughout your nursing career. After completing your nursing programme, you will register with the NMC to practice as a nurse in the UK. Annual registration fees are currently £120, something to bear in mind for the future.

Activity 3.4: Further research into the NMC

To learn more about the NMC. Go to YouTube and find a short video titled About the Nursing and Midwifery Council by NMCVideos: https://youtu.be/gXaZ2U_BuoE.

It is a short animation explaining the NMC's role and why it matters to everyone.

Questions

- *Who does the NMC regulate?*
- *What is the role of the NMC in terms of nurse education?*
- *What is revalidation, and how often does it need to be completed?*

A suggested answer is given at the end of the chapter.

The NMC (2021) requires all nurses and midwives to undergo revalidation every three years in order to renew their registration. Revalidation is the process of demonstrating that you practice safely and effectively. It has several parts, including a reflective discussion, engagement with professional development and a minimum number of practice hours. While revalidation is still a few years away, awareness of the process may help you appreciate the lifelong learning commitment of being a nurse. The NMC is an integral part of nursing, and as a future nurse, you will become familiar with this organisation during your studies.

Conclusion

As the first day of your studies approaches, this chapter has introduced areas that will help you prepare for success. Understanding the complexities of the available funding options will ensure you receive appropriate financial support. You should feel clearer about the funding arrangements for student nurses and how to keep within budget once you start the course. This chapter has provided information about recommended reading resources, and you can check the list at the end of the chapter for texts that may be worth considering. We have also given further details on the equipment you will encounter during the early stages of your course. The vital role that the NMC standards play in terms of nurse education has been set out. Remember that thorough preparation is more than just easing initial nerves; it lays the groundwork for making a sound start to your studies. In the next chapter, we will guide you through the transition into becoming a student nurse as you commence your studies.

Suggested answers

Activity 3.1

At the time of writing, £8,400 is the maximum Maintenance Loan available.

How much you are eligible for will depend upon your circumstances. Try using the figure when completing activity 3.2.

Scenario: Aishah

Aishah might consider how much she could save by living at home in Bristol. She could compare and contrast this with the financial support available to nursing students in Wales and Scotland and other options for bringing in income, such as part-time work. Aishah may also think about the cost of tuition and how this would be met, which could differ between universities. Ultimately, her choice may be influenced by a compromise between financial considerations and the experiences she will gain from studying nursing away from home.

Activity 3.2

Completing the Financial Health Check activity can help you progress more effectively during your studies in various ways. To begin with, understanding your financial situation and having a clear budget can reduce financial stress and uncertainty. This will enable you to concentrate on your studies rather than undue worry over money. By managing your finances proactively, you can avoid unexpected financial difficulties impacting your studies. Anticipating and planning for expenses such as books, supplies, transportation, and accommodation can help ensure these are taken care of. This activity can also promote responsible financial habits, which can be beneficial during your university years and once you qualify as a nurse.

Activity 3.3

- The BMJ Best Practice app provides evidence-based information on various medical conditions and treatment options.
- BNF Publications provides healthcare professionals with medicines information.
- The British Red Cross First Aid site offers step-by-step instructions and videos for different first aid scenarios, which can be helpful for clinical placements.
- NHS App provides access to health advice, appointment booking, prescription ordering, and other services.

Activity 3.4

Who does the NMC regulate? Nurses, Midwives and Nursing Associates

What is the role of the NMC in terms of nurse education? The NMC is responsible for setting education standards and approving educational institutions and programmes. They also ensure that approved programmes and practice placements are of high quality.

What is revalidation, and how often does it need to be completed? Revalidation involves evidencing continual learning, development, and reflection. It needs to be completed every three years.

Recommended reading

Alexander's Nursing Practice: Hospital and Home, edited by Ian Peate (2019), provides the knowledge and skills needed for competent, evidence-based nursing practice in a variety of settings.

The Language of Kindness: A Nurse's Story is Christie Watson's (2018) memoir which shares her 20-year experience as a nurse, opening the doors to the hospital and sharing its secrets, joys, and challenges.

Clinical Pocket Reference by Bernie Garrett, Paul Ong and Paul Galdas (2022) provides key information that a nurse will need on placement and in practice, chosen by experienced teachers and practitioners.

Essentials of Nursing Practice, edited by Catherine Delves-Yates (2022), is a definitive textbook that introduces the core topics and information that every nursing student will need to master during their degree.

The Student Nurse Handbook by Bethann Siviter (2013) is now a decade old but still provides a valuable guide for student nurses, covering everything from academic work and placements to student well-being and managing finances.

Useful websites

Nursing and Midwifery Council is the professional regulatory body for nurses and midwives in the UK. Their site provides information on standards, codes of practice, revalidation, and more. ***https://www.nmc.org.uk/***

Royal College of Nursing provides information on how to become a nurse, including qualifications needed, where to study, and advice on beginning your nursing career. ***https://www.rcn.org.uk/Professional-Development/become-a-nurse***

The Student Room offers tips and advice for students, including articles for student nurses. ***https://www.thestudentroom.co.uk/university/advice/the-five-things-you-must-do-before-starting-your-nursing-course***

UCAS provides information on nursing course entry requirements, applying with a degree, and interview tips. ***https://www.ucas.com/explore/subjects/nursing***

THE TRANSITION

Introduction

The transition to university can be both exciting and daunting. It is a transformative step not only in your education but also in terms of life in general. It is a time of new experiences, curiosity, and a degree of trepidation. This chapter is designed to help you navigate this transition. You will likely have many questions during the early stages of your nurse education. We will try to help you with these, starting with an examination of what to expect during the first few days and weeks of university. We will explain how university works and introduce you to the structures that shape academia. There will be consideration of undertaking paid work while studying, a common experience for nursing students. The chapter will then explore the theory and practice you will likely encounter during the early stages of the course, including patient-centred care, clinical skills, and the development of therapeutic relationships. As you start this new chapter of your life, the challenges and experiences you gain will mould you into a capable, compassionate nurse in the future.

The first days and weeks

As a student nurse, studying at university will likely differ from anything you have experienced in your educational journey. This fact still applies even if you have previously studied another topic at university due to the unique mix of academic, professional, and practice requirements inherent to nursing. In contrast to school or college, university is a more autonomous environment. You will be expected to take ownership of your learning and independently manage aspects of your educational journey.

Before the teaching starts, you will go through a period of induction and have the opportunity to participate in freshers' week. The week is designed to serve as a bridge for new students, easing their transition into university life. It is usually packed with activities and events designed to help you settle in, make friends, and become acquainted with your new academic and social environment (Student Information Scotland, 2020). Freshers' week offers a plethora of social opportunities. You are likely to have the chance to find out about university clubs and societies that will entice you to join. These societies are excellent places to pursue your interests, make friends, and have memorable university experiences. Freshers' week typically includes various social events such as parties, movie nights, city tours, quizzes, and themed events. These events encourage you to interact with other students and immerse yourself in the university's social life. Staying safe during freshers' week is essential, especially as you may find yourself in new situations and unfamiliar surroundings (Complete University Guide, 2023b). Be sure to eat well and stay responsible if drinking on nights out. It is essential to watch your bottle or glass to prevent it from being spiked, the act of drugs or alcohol being added to a person's drink without their knowledge or consent. Take a trusted taxi or university bus service to get home late at night with friends. These simple steps can help you maintain your safety, and it is recommended that you look out for other tips and advice from your university or student association.

Freshers' week also involves campus tours, information sessions, social events, and club fairs. There will be a period of induction during which you will receive information about academic expectations, the structure of your course and the support services available. You may also have introductory meetings with your programme leaders and lecturers. An early official event is the registration process, where you formally become a student and enrol in the course. This is a vital step as it confirms your place and is often linked to accommodation arrangements and the use of university IT systems. During this process, you will likely receive your student ID card, enabling you to utilise university facilities such as the library. If you have a disability, accessing support via student services as early as possible during your studies is essential. They will assist you in navigating the challenges of higher education while focusing on your studies. Disability advisors and counsellors can help find and implement appropriate accommodations and services that will enable you to engage in university life (Stacey, 2022). Accessing support from an early stage may also help promote belonging within the university community. Find out more about disability services in Chapter 5.

Activity 4.1: Reflection and Journaling

During the few weeks of your transition to university, you will be on a steep learning curve. A reflective journal can help you navigate this learning process and keep things manageable. The primary goal of this activity is to provide a structured environment to process all the new information, thoughts, and feelings. Journaling should take approximately 30 minutes per day, preferably in the evening. During this time, you will reflect on the day's events, noting what you have learned and any questions that have arisen. You should also write down your feelings or thoughts during these experiences. By providing an outlet for self-expression, this daily journaling will help you consolidate all the new information you will encounter during the first few weeks, clarify areas of uncertainty, and manage stress levels. It also allows you to track your emotional responses and how well you handle situations, providing valuable insights into your progress and areas where you may benefit from seeking support. As a daily habit, you should find the reflective process beneficial, and it could be something to consider continuing after the first few weeks of the process. Beginning a nursing programme is an exciting but challenging time that will be filled with a wide range of emotions and experiences. It is helpful to remember that there will be ups and downs, a normal part of the process for all students embarking on this new endeavour.

Questions

- *Which experiences or topics did you find most challenging after one week of journaling, and why?*
- *How have your emotions and stress levels changed over the first week?*

A suggested answer is given at the end of the chapter.

Once the induction period has finished, you will then start with teaching and learning. During the first stages of the programme, you will likely find that you learn about the nursing profession. You will typically learn in lectures, seminars, simulation/skills, or workshops during the start of your studies, with clinical placements taking place later in year one. There will be opportunities to meet your classmates, each of whom will bring different experiences and perspectives. Your lecturers and tutors will likely set up activities so you can get to know one another better. These connections can provide mutual support and learning, with group study sessions, projects, and socialising helping you to develop bonds with others. You will also get to know your lecturers, who will provide a great deal of advice and information.

The first few weeks of your nurse education will be intense. You will be expected to learn a wide range of topics while becoming familiar with university systems and other aspects of your transition. Please know that feeling overwhelmed during the first few weeks of your nursing programme is perfectly normal. The demands of the coursework, adjusting to new environments, balancing academic and personal life, and the weight of future responsibilities are common challenges experienced by nursing students (Pryjmachuk et al., 2019). While the journey may appear daunting, keep in mind that every nursing student before you has been down a similar road. What seems overwhelming will gradually become familiar, and what appears impossible will become second nature. The key is to stay motivated, be open to learning, and remind yourself why you chose nursing. Starting nursing is like learning a new language; there are so many new words and terms you have never heard before. This unfamiliarity can knock your confidence, especially if you mispronounce them in class or during an early placement. Like any language, you will struggle to begin with, but within six months you will be using these words without a second thought. By the end of your studies, you will be pretty much fluent!

How university works

The academic year runs from September to June and is usually divided into three terms, Autumn, Spring and Summer. Each term is approximately 10-12 weeks, with breaks and assessment periods in between. This structure allows you to have a period of study, take assessments, and then have a gap before the next term start. It is worth being aware that some universities have intakes at other times of the year. Due to course content and placement hours needed, nursing students will often have studies throughout the year, even when the rest of the university is quiet!

One of the key terms you will come across as you begin your university journey is the term 'module'. Your degree programme is divided into smaller units of study known as modules. Each module focuses on a topic, giving you a thorough understanding of that subject or a combination of subjects. Modules are worth credits which are typically earned by completing and passing the associated coursework and assessments (Quality Assurance Agency for Higher Education, 2021). The credits are added together as you progress through your studies. Modules can be worth different amounts, but the number of credits needed for each stage of your programme will be fixed. Usually, you will need 120 credits for each level (or year if studying full-time) to meet the requirements. So, this would require you to complete six 20-credit modules. If you are studying over three years, you will complete a total of 360 credits at the various levels to be awarded your degree. See the concept box for more information.

The specific credit requirements and the distribution of credits may vary between universities. Assessments are an essential component of the module structure. Each nursing module will have its own evaluation criteria, which may include a mix of written or oral assignments, presentations, practical assessments, Objective

Structured Clinical Examinations (OSCEs), and exams.

Concept box: University Credits

The UK higher education credit framework works based on the Credit Accumulation and Transfer Scheme (CATS). The credit system is beneficial because it provides a standardised method of comparing the workload of different courses and qualifications, making it easier for students to transfer between various universities or programmes. Here are a few specifics about university credits:

- *1 credit roughly equates to 10 hours of total work, including contact hours (time spent in lectures, seminars, and practical sessions) and independent study.*
- *A typical undergraduate degree (Bachelor's) requires 360 credits, achieved over three years of full-time study (120 credits per year).*
- *An undergraduate honours degree usually requires 480 credits, typically achieved over four years of full-time study (120 credits per year).*
- *Postgraduate certificates generally require 60 credits, postgraduate diplomas require 120 credits, and a master's degree usually requires 180 credits.*

It is important to note that these figures may differ depending on the university and programme.

These assessments assess your knowledge and understanding and the development of other nursing competencies and proficiencies. You will learn at your own pace, and do not expect everything to fall into place immediately. Remember that your nursing programme is a marathon, not a race.

Working while studying

Working while studying to become a nurse has its benefits and drawbacks. Many nursing students must work to help cover their living costs and other expenses (Salamonson et al., 2018). They can also gain valuable experience if working in a health and social care setting (Wise, Ossenberg and Henderson, 2022). Working while studying can also help expand your professional network, and you may have experienced colleagues who can offer advice and support. Despite these benefits, working while studying nursing has some drawbacks. Taking on significant work as a nursing student alongside studying can negatively impact engagement and academic achievement (Christiansen et al., 2019; Christiansen et al., 2020). Nursing programmes are frequently demanding, requiring significant study. You will be attending regular classes and completing complex assessments during your studies. While on placement, you will often be on shifts a full 37.5 hrs per week. These placement hours can make it difficult to hold down another job without the help of flexible working or an understanding boss!

Excessive work alongside study also brings the real risk of additional stress and potential burnout. It can lead to long days with little time for rest or relaxation. This can quickly lead to physical and mental exhaustion, which has a knock-on effect on your academic studies and work (Salamonson et al., 2020). You may also miss out on social activities and group study opportunities, which can impact emotional well-being and lead to feelings of isolation. Furthermore, there may be little time for self-care, which can have a negative impact on both physical and mental health (Salamonson et al., 2018). It is, therefore, essential that you manage your time carefully. Discuss your studies early on with your employer and explain the support you need. Ensure that they understand that your studies are important to you. Agree on a manageable workload and tell your employer that there will be limited opportunities for you to work during placements. Avoid getting caught in a cycle of covering shifts and not attending classes to work. This situation will be detrimental to your studies and may also impact your well-being.

Patient-centred care

Patient-centred care is an essential concept in nursing. Understanding and applying this concept as a nursing student will be vital to your development during the early stages of your studies. Patient-centred care is when healthcare workers respect patients' preferences, needs, and values. Patient-centred care places the patient into the driving seat of their care. Rather than passive recipients, they are supported to be active participants in their care. This model of care can improve patient satisfaction, health outcomes and even reduce healthcare costs. Understanding each patient as an individual is a central aspect of patient-centred care. You should incorporate a person's unique experiences, values, and beliefs into their care plan to achieve this.

> ***Student insights***
>
> *"Patient-centred care is to consider all physical, psychological and mental needs of patient and provide the best comprehensive care for [them]."*
>
> *Student nurse research participant*
>
> *(Ghane and Esmaeili, 2020, p.385)*

As a student nurse, you frequently spend more time with the patient than other professionals. Engaging with patients can provide insights into each individual and their unique character and needs. It is essential to allow patients to express their concerns, fears and hopes about their health. Providing clear and understandable information will help patients make decisions about their care. Patient-centred care also includes involving the patient's family and support network as appropriate. Family and friends can offer additional support, insight, and information, which can improve patient-centred care. Patient-centred care is supported through effective teamwork and communication, helping to ensure that care is delivered seamlessly.

Clinical skills

Regardless of their field, nurses must show they are proficient in a range of core clinical skills (NMC, 2018c). These competencies help to ensure that patients receive safe and high-quality. During your first year, you will learn these skills in modules designed to help you prepare for your initial placements. These will usually be delivered alongside other learning about nursing values and foundational theory (e.g. anatomy and physiology). The following sections will introduce you to the clinical skills you will likely cover.

Patient assessment

Patient assessment is a crucial nursing skill that entails observing and assessing a patient's condition. It involves conducting health interviews and performing physical examinations. You will also learn to take vital signs such as blood pressure, temperature, pulse, and respiration rate. These assessments provide helpful information needed to plan and deliver individualised care to each patient. As a first-year nursing student, you will be taught how to conduct these assessments systematically while demonstrating compassion and respect (Clarke, 2014). Careful observation is at the heart of patient assessment. Your observation skills can lead to early detection of changes in a patient's condition, inform care, and improve patient outcomes. Physical assessment will include vital signs such as heart rate, blood pressure, temperature, and respiratory rate. You will also learn to evaluate many other areas, such as the patient's responsiveness and pain levels (Haugh, 2015). Open-ended questions can encourage patients to share their experiences in their own words, providing you with valuable insights during the assessment. You should consider the patient's mental and emotional state in your assessment. Any signs of anxiety, depression, or other mental health issues must be identified because they can significantly impact a patient's physical health and recovery.

Activity 4.2: Patient assessment

This activity is intended to help you gain a better understanding of patient assessment techniques as well as to foster empathy. It will encourage you to consider the questions you ask patients, your assessment techniques, and how these interactions may affect the patient.

Instructions:

Begin by sitting comfortably in a quiet location where you can focus. Close your eyes and visualise yourself in a medical setting, such as a hospital or clinic. Now imagine yourself as a patient rather than a nurse. You have come in for a general check-up. Imagine being asked about your medical history and detailed questions about your current health. Consider how these questions would make you feel. Would they bother you in any way? Write down your emotional responses to these questions. Consider them and ask yourself why they made you feel this way. Is there anything the nurse could do to make you feel more comfortable? Now consider the physical part of the assessment. How would you feel as the nurse examines your vital signs by taking your pulse and checking your breathing? Would certain aspects of the assessment make you feel uneasy? How can the nurse make the procedure more pleasant and less stressful for you?

Having completed this activity, you have put yourself in a patient's shoes rather than your professional ones. It may have helped you develop empathy and understanding of the patient experience. Try reflecting on your reactions during this activity to help inform your practice when conducting patient assessments during your placements.

Question

- *Spend time making a list of ways to make your questions and assessment techniques more comfortable for your patients.*

A suggested answer is given at the end of the chapter.

Critical thinking is woven into all stages of patient assessment. You will be expected to synthesise and interpret the information you collect, drawing on your knowledge to connect a patient's symptoms and the required care (Westerdahl et al., 2020). Accurate and timely documentation is an essential component of patient assessment. It ensures that all healthcare team members access the same information, promoting continuity and care. The documentation also ensures a record of the patient's health and the care you provided. As you progress through your nurse education, you will improve your assessment skills and clinical judgement.

Activities of daily living

Another aspect of nursing involves supporting people with their activities of daily living. These include areas such as assistance with personal hygiene, eating, drinking, using the toilet, and mobilising (Osakwe et al., 2017). When it comes to eating and drinking, your role will extend beyond providing food and drink. You will need to ensure patients get enough nutrition and water while promoting their independence. It will require familiarity with dietary requirements and how different health conditions affect a patient's ability to eat and drink. Throughout your first year and beyond, you will discover that these fundamental aspects of patient care provide valuable opportunities to connect with patients and understand their needs. They may appear simple, but these tasks often significantly impact a patient's quality of life.

Scenario: Camila

Imagine you are in your first placement in a stroke ward. Camila, 52, was admitted to the stroke unit a few days ago after a right-sided cerebrovascular accident (CVA). A CVA, often known as a stroke, occurs when the blood supply to a part of the brain is cut off or reduced, preventing brain tissue from receiving oxygen and nutrients and thus causing brain cells to die. The CVA has caused significant weakness in her left side and communication difficulties. You entered Camila's room around dinner time to check her feelings. While in the room, you see a full plate of food and a drink on her tray, both still warm but completely untouched. Camila's stroke has left her with difficulty using her left hand, making it hard for her to feed herself. You recognise the importance of ensuring Camila receives adequate nutrition and hydration but do not know much about her health status.

Question

- *Should you start assisting Camila with eating and drinking the items on the tray?*

A suggested answer is given at the end of the chapter.

As a student nurse, you may assist patients with personal care and toilet use. Providing such care transforms a private, individual activity into a social process (Thompson et al., 2021). Respect is demonstrated by knocking on the door and waiting for a response before you enter. Privacy and dignity are paramount when supporting patients with personal care. You should begin by closing the door and drawing the curtains to create a private space. Communication with the patient is important, explaining the support you will be providing and obtaining their consent. Appropriate draping and physical support can help protect modesty; remember that small things matter (Social Care Institute for Excellence, 2020). During vulnerable times, eye contact and reassuring communication foster trust. It is equally important to use respectful language and keep discussions private. These practices demonstrate nurses' dedication to promoting privacy and dignity, thereby improving the patient's overall experience.

Infection control

Nurses must follow strict hygiene protocols and infection control measures to ensure patient safety. Infection control is essential in nursing and all other healthcare professions. As a first-year nursing student, you will need to become familiar with infection prevention and control principles. Infection control involves preventing healthcare-associated infections and is a vital aspect of patient safety. Hand hygiene is perhaps the most fundamental component of infection control. The World Health Organisation (WHO) (2009) has produced Your 5 Moments for Hand Hygiene (see figure 4.1). This sets out that you should carry out hand hygiene before touching a patient, before clean/aseptic procedure, after body fluid exposure

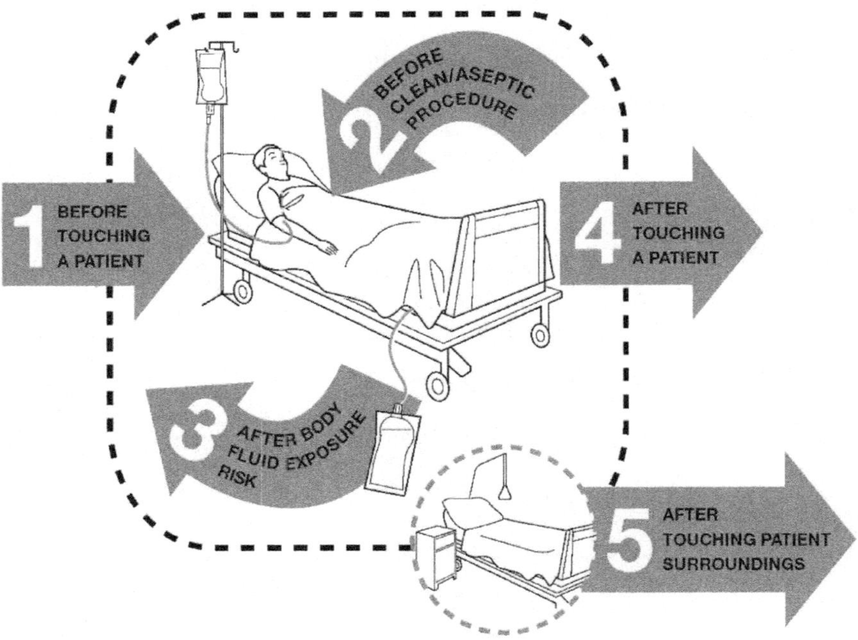

Figure 4.1: Reproduced from 5 Moments for Hand Hygiene, WHO (2009).

risk, after touching a patient, and after touching patient surroundings. Depending on the situation, nurses should either use soap and water or hand rub to adhere to these principles.

Personal protective equipment (PPE) is another area to learn about. Depending on the situation, gloves, gowns, masks, and eye protection may all be required. To prevent contamination and the spread of infection, proper donning (putting on) and doffing (taking off) of PPE is essential. When caring for patients with certain types of infections, isolation precautions must be taken. Cleaning and sterilisation can assist in preventing the spread of pathogens. These techniques include routine cleaning, equipment sterilisation and the decontamination of the patient environment. Different levels of disinfection or sterilisation may be required depending on the level of risk. You will also learn about broader aspects of infection control, such as healthcare worker immunisation, surveillance for healthcare-associated infections, and antibiotic stewardship. As a first-year nursing student, you will need to demonstrate an understanding of infection control precautions and put them into practice during clinical placements. Remember that everyone has a role in infection control, and nurses are often at the forefront of promoting a safe culture and preventing infections in healthcare settings.

Medicine management:

Medicine management entails a wide range of responsibilities and starts with understanding the medications used. You will learn about the types of drugs used and how they affect the patient. Over time you will become familiar with typical dosages, administration routes and potential side effects. This knowledge will help you understand prescriptions, provide patient education and monitor patients for possible drug reactions. One area to begin learning is the 'five rights' or '5 Rs' of medication administration, which consists of the right patient, medication, dose, route, and time (Pearce, 2021). By adhering to these five rights, you can play a role in reducing medication errors, ensuring patient safety, and improving the effectiveness of medication. It is also essential that patient allergies are checked before administration of a medicine. There are many legal and ethical issues associated with this skill. These include considerations such as informed consent and the right of patients to refuse medication.

Activity 4.3: Medicine of the week

This activity aims to become familiar with various medications over time. You will do this by utilising the extensive and reliable resources the British National Formulary (BNF) provides. Healthcare professionals use the BNF to review information about the many medications available, such as how they should be used, what they are for, and any potential side effects. To begin this activity, you must first gain access to the BNF by downloading and installing the app (see Activity 3.3) on your smartphone or tablet. If you prefer a more tactile learning experience, a paper copy of the formulary may be worth investing in. You can often pick up second-hand copies at a low cost. These are useful for learning purposes but are usually not the most current version and should not be used in practice with actual patients.

Your task is simple but effective. Every Monday, as a new week begins, go through your BNF, whether digitally or physically, and randomly choose a medication associated with your field of nursing. You will then take time to get to know this medicine over the next week. You should decipher its characteristics, uses, potential side effects, and contraindications, laying the groundwork to inform your nursing practice. Once the next week comes around, choose a new medicine and repeat the same process. This weekly exploration will provide a regular introduction to new medications and a deeper understanding of nursing pharmacology. This knowledge of different medicines will be especially beneficial when in placement.

Questions

- *Do you believe this activity will improve your ability to communicate medication information to patients or other healthcare professionals?*
- *Would you recommend this activity to other nursing students?*

A suggested answer is given at the end of the chapter.

You should always be appropriately supervised when administering drugs (Pearce, 2021). Additionally, you will have undertaken theoretical learning before participating in this skill. Check with your university if you are unsure about your role in medicine administration. Following administration, ensure that you monitor the patient to watch for any expected effects, potential side effects, or adverse reactions. If any adverse events occur, quickly report these to a more senior nurse so that appropriate measures can be taken. It is essential to be aware of your responsibilities when it comes to accurately documenting the medicine administration and other details (NMC, 2018a). Many healthcare providers are now moving towards electronic rather than paper records, so you may need login details to allow you to carry out this aspect of the procedure. If the patient refuses medication, this must also be documented and reported.

Medicine management requires a combination of knowledge and skills you will develop throughout your nurse education. Safe and effective medicine management is more than just performing tasks correctly. It is also about understanding the 'why' behind each aspect of the procedure.

Communication and therapeutic relationships

Communication skills are essential to the provision of safe, effective, and compassionate nursing care. Listening, speaking clearly, and explaining information straightforwardly will enhance the patient experience (McKenna et al., 2020). It will also help to ensure that you demonstrate empathy and respect. Nursing communication requires you to develop relationships, establish trust, and create an environment where patients feel safe and cared for. These are central to an effective 'therapeutic relationship', something you can learn about in the concept box. Good communication can improve patient outcomes, increase patient satisfaction, and result in fewer errors.

Concept box: Therapeutic relationship

Therapeutic relationships are a crucial concept for effective nursing practice. It is an interpersonal relationship through which the nurse and patient work together towards improving the person's health and well-being. Respect for the patient's autonomy is essential in fostering a therapeutic relationship. It often begins through the establishment of rapport and trust. This starts with the first encounter when you create a welcoming environment to encourage open communication. The way you introduce yourself, the attention you give to the patient's comfort, and your demonstration of professionalism are all important. Displaying empathy through understanding the patient's feelings, thoughts, and experiences will help develop the therapeutic relationship further (Moreno-Poyato and Rodríguez-Nogueira, 2021). Use your communication skills to ask relevant questions and actively listen while retaining professional boundaries. Sometimes body language, facial expressions, and tone of voice matter more than words.

As a nursing student, you must become proficient in various communication styles. Verbal communication encompasses what you say and how you say it. Speaking clearly and using simple language can help ensure the patient understands the information. Remember to recognise cultural diversity in communication styles, inclusive of non-verbal cues (Sensenig, 2022). Body language, facial expressions, and even silence all convey powerful messages. Active listening shows respect and ensures the patient's wishes and needs are considered (McKenna et al., 2020). Remember that communication is not limited to interactions with patients. You will be part of a multidisciplinary team and must display effective communication with other health and social care professionals. This approach involves clearly and concisely providing information about a patient in a structured manner while actively listening to other team members (Stevens, McNiesh and Goyal, 2020). It is essential to have a respectful, collaborative attitude to contribute to effective team working.

Conclusion

The transition to university is a significant milestone that marks the start of an exciting journey. The first few days and weeks are crucial, as they often set the tone for the rest of the university experience. It is a period of adjustment to new surroundings and people. In this chapter, we have explored how university works and some of the main areas that you will learn about during the early stages of your studies. Take advantage of induction events, and do not be afraid to seek advice from lecturers, student services, and experienced students. If you need to undertake paid work while you study, discussing and planning how your employer can support you during your nurse education is vital. You have been introduced to essential features of nurse education you will likely encounter during the early stages of your course, including patient assessment, infection control and medicine management. Developing clinical skills takes time and practice, so be patient and allow your knowledge and understanding to deepen over time. Starting your studies is a significant step towards becoming a nurse. Approach this transition with an open mind and be ready to face the challenges and opportunities that lie ahead.

Suggested answers

Activity 4.1

During the first few weeks of journaling, you may have found some aspects of your nursing studies more difficult than others. There are probably many different university systems and processes to become familiar with, which can initially seem overwhelming. You will also have been meeting new classmates and lecturers, and relationships can take time to establish. Then there is the terminology used in academia and nursing that you may not have encountered previously. Getting to grips with the complexities of patient care and the healthcare system may have posed challenges. Recognising and exploring these experiences is the first step towards overcoming them. It will help organise your thoughts and enable you to seek additional information and guidance to support your transition.

You may have noticed patterns emerging when you reflect on your emotions and stress levels. It is possible that you felt more stressed on days when you had full days of sessions. Perhaps you felt anxious when studying unfamiliar or complex topics or relieved and satisfied after completing specific tasks. The interpersonal aspect of meeting new people and developing friendships is likely to have an emotional impact. The journaling may help you identify stress triggers, providing opportunities to develop coping strategies for these specific situations. It may help you understand and manage your emotions and stress as you settle into your nursing studies.

Activity 4.2

Making assessments and asking questions in a healthcare setting can be intimidating for patients. Here are some areas you may have thought about when considering how to make these procedures more comfortable:

- Introduce yourself: Clearly introduce yourself by your full name and professional title so the patient understands who you are and your role in their care.
- Ask how the person would like to be addressed: Some people prefer to be addressed by their first name, while others prefer a more formal approach. Inquiring demonstrates respect for the patient's personal preferences.
- Use active listening: Demonstrate that you are fully engaged and interested in what the patient is saying by nodding, maintaining eye contact, and summarising their statements as needed.
- Personal space: Be aware of and respectful of the patient's personal space, as it varies significantly between individuals.
- Allow enough time: Do not rush the patient through their responses. Allow plenty of time for them to think and respond.
- Avoid interruptions: If possible, avoid interruptions such as phone calls or other distractions during the assessment.

Scenario: Camila

The short answer is no. Difficulty swallowing, or dysphagia, is common in stroke patients. Patients who have problems swallowing require close supervision and assistance to avoid choking or aspiration. It is important that during your early placement experiences, you do not proceed with assisting a person to eat or drink until you have established that they do not have any swallowing difficulties. Discuss Camila's needs with your Practice Supervisor or another nurse before you start assisting her. Ensure that you act promptly and keep Camila updated. Check the patient's notes carefully and find out information from Camila and her family as appropriate. Once it has been established that it is safe to proceed, you must explain what you are doing and promote Camila's independence as far as possible.

Activity 4.3

You may have discovered that understanding medications better can help you communicate their use to patients and healthcare professionals. This activity provides factual information about each medicine and encourages critical thinking about its uses, side effects, and interactions. This understanding may enable you to communicate information in a patient-friendly manner, ensuring that they fully understand their treatment. It also allows more informed conversations with other healthcare professionals, promoting a collaborative approach to patient care.

This activity could benefit any nursing student looking to improve their understanding of pharmacology. It encourages self-directed, continuous learning, an essential skill in the ever-changing healthcare field. The activity provides an in-depth view without being overwhelming because it focuses on one medication per week, making it a manageable and effective learning tool. With all this in mind, suggesting this activity to other nursing students may be worthwhile to help them on their learning journey.

Recommended reading

Fundamentals of Person-Centred Healthcare Practice: A Guide for Healthcare Students edited by Brendan McCormack et al. (2021), provides evidence-based perspectives related to the concept of person-centred care.

Ross and Wilson's Anatomy and Physiology in Health and Illness by Anne Waugh and Allison Grant (2018) provides a solid foundation in anatomy and physiology, which is crucial for nursing students.

Royal Marsden Manual of Clinical Nursing Procedures**,** Student Edition, edited by Lister et al. (2021), has been written specifically for student nurses and covers a wide range of clinical nursing procedures.

Useful websites

Nurse.org.uk is a site offering a collection of resources for nurses, including articles, a directory of nursing schools, and a forum for nurses to connect.

Nurses.co.uk is a comprehensive website offering nursing news, career tips, and online learning resources for nurses in the UK. It includes a blog post sharing five tips for student nurses entering their first year of a degree:

StudentNurseProject.wordpress.com is a great resource run by nursing students and newly registered nurses. They provide blogs, study tips, and insights into different areas of nursing.

ACHIEVING SUCCESS

Introduction

Balancing education, personal responsibilities, and self-care takes a lot of effort. This chapter will take a holistic approach to balancing various aspects of study and life so that you can achieve success. It will start by considering specific NMC requirements you must meet during your studies. We will then explore how you can pass your assessments by considering tips and techniques designed to help with essays and group work projects. We will also discuss tools and strategies to assist you in planning, prioritising, and utilising your time effectively. Undertaking your nurse education will be busy and, at times, intense. Planning a healthy schedule and dividing tasks will help manage workload and avoid burnout. This chapter will also consider a challenge that virtually all student nurses will face at some point during their studies: procrastination. It is easy to put off tasks until the last minute, but doing so can result in unnecessary stress and poor performance. We will consider ways to overcome procrastination. There is also a discussion on the responsible use of social media provided. The final section of this chapter explores how you can maintain your health and well-being through self-care. By considering these strategies for success, you are developing essential skills that will serve you well as a student and throughout your nursing career.

Meeting NMC requirements

The NMC Future nurse standards offer a foundation of knowledge and skills that promote person-centred, holistic care (Holt and Dixon, 2022). These set out the knowledge and skills that student nurses from any of the four fields must demonstrate to join the NMC register.

The NMC (2018c) has established proficiency standards for registered nurses, which set out the skills, knowledge, and characteristics to provide safe and effective care. The proficiencies are grouped under seven platforms: Annex A and Annex B. Annex A focuses on communication and relationship management skills. It specifies the essential communication skills registered nurses must demonstrate to establish effective connections with colleagues and maintain therapeutic relationships with patients and families. Here are some examples of the NMC (2018c) skills that need to be achieved during your course:

- Active listening and responding appropriately to verbal and non-verbal cues.
- Demonstrating empathy, compassion, and respect in all interactions.
- Adapting communication styles to meet the needs of diverse populations, including those with communication difficulties or sensory impairments.
- Using appropriate language and terminology when discussing sensitive issues or providing information about care and treatment options.
- Collaborating effectively with interprofessional teams to ensure coordinated care and support for patients and their families.

Annex B outlines eleven nursing procedures that registered nurses must be able to demonstrate to provide compassionate, evidence-based, person-centred nursing care. Here are some examples of the NMC (2018c) procedures that need to be achieved during your course:

- Techniques to undertake and interpret vital signs, venepuncture, blood sampling, ECGs, and blood transfusions.
- Management of medical devices such as cardiac monitors, infusion pumps, and measurement of weight, height, and

BMI.

- Interventions and assessments related to pain management, privacy, skin care, wound care, and aseptic techniques.
- Evidence-based approaches to assess mental health, including signs of distress, cognitive impairment, and suicidal ideation.
- Procedures for assessing and optimising nutrition, hydration, bladder, and bowel health.

To achieve these proficiencies, you will combine theoretical and practical learning experiences, including practice placements, simulation, and interprofessional education. Each day will present opportunities to make small steps forward towards proficiency. The path is not always straight, but each interaction, task, and team collaboration you engage in will make a small contribution to your development. There will be days when your communication skills shine and others when your decision-making abilities are tested. The key is to reflect on these experiences regularly, analysing what went well and where improvements can be made. This active participation in reflection will enhance your learning and proficiency development. Seeking constructive feedback from Practice Assessors, Practice Supervisors, academic staff, and peers will help you make progress. They give you new perspectives, broaden your understanding, and point you in the right direction. Receiving and incorporating feedback will gradually shape you into a skilled, knowledgeable, compassionate nurse.

Passing assessments

Passing your assessments will no doubt be at the top of your mind to support your progression through your studies. Although many of the tips in this chapter will help you maximise your ability to do as well as possible, there are a few specific areas to be aware of. In the following sections, we will look at how you can do well in a couple of common types of assessment within nursing programmes, the essay and group project. We will also consider how to use feedback to fast-track your development.

Tips for essays

Becoming adept at essay writing will be essential to your development as a student nurse. It entails several crucial procedures, from knowing the assessment requirements to correctly identifying sources. A clear and well-structured essay indicates you have understood a specific topic and demonstrates your ability to link theory to practice.

Understanding the assessment criteria is your first step. Before you begin writing, ensure you understand what the essay is asking for and what you should offer. What are the main points or questions? What types of arguments or evidence should be expected? A firm grasp of these issues can influence your research and writing processes (University of Oxford, 2023). Check for information and presentations that your lecturers have provided on the module site and spend time familiarising yourself with the assessment requirements. The writing and editing processes can then begin. Start with an initial essay plan with a clear introduction, body, and conclusion. The introduction should include a quick overview of the topic of the essay, the body should concentrate on your arguments and evidence, and the conclusion should summarise your results. Then, divide the overall word count into parts of the essay so you know how much to write in each section. If marks are available for each section, you can use this to help calculate the number of words that should be used. Ensure you follow the assessment guidelines carefully, as there can be penalties for going significantly over or under the word count.

Activity 5.1: Unpacking the Essay Question

This activity is intended to help you understand and unpack essay questions, an essential first step in any successful essay-writing process. It will help you to strategise your development and writing process to construct a more focused essay.

First, find a quiet place to concentrate and carefully read the essay question. Libraries will often provide spaces that are conducive to study. Remember that understanding an essay question requires reading and understanding what it asks you to do. Now determine the question's keywords. These could be words related to the topic you must cover, such as a particular nursing theory or patient care approach. Look for words that indicate the type of response required - words like 'analyse,' 'discuss,' 'compare,' or 'evaluate' provide hints about the depth and breadth of the response expected. Many universities will explain the different terms used in assessment criteria – ask academic services for details. Once you have identified the keywords, write them down and consider what they mean. For example, if the question instructs you to 'compare' two nursing models, you must discuss their similarities and differences. If the question is complicated, divide it into smaller parts. Essay questions often have multiple factors that must be addressed. List how you intend to approach each section and the points you plan to cover. Finally, create a brief initial plan for your essay based on your understanding of the question. This could include the main points you will cover and any arguments to be set out. Remember that this is only a starting point that will change as you progress with your essay.

Questions

- *How can this approach to unpacking an essay question be extended to other types of assessment that you will undertake during your studies?*
- *How will you approach essay questions differently in the future as a result of this activity?*

A suggested answer is given at the end of the chapter.

Writing an essay will often entail several drafts. Do not be overly concerned about the quality of the first draft – the goal is to get your ideas down in a logical order. During the editing process, you can revise and polish your work by assessing it for clarity, coherence, and relevance (Emery, 2014). Always provide enough time to proofread your essay before submitting it. This stage includes checking for spelling and grammar issues and confirming the accuracy and relevance of your text. Stepping away from your essay for a day or two before revising it can give you fresh eyes to spot faults or gaps in your reasoning. Using up-to-date, reliable, and credible evidence efficiently is crucial in nursing. Remember you will be applying the theory to practice, so you need to know that the measures used with patients are supported by appropriate evidence. Always back up your statements and arguments with relevant evidence from academic and professional sources. This will improve the quality of your discussion and exhibit your knowledge of the subject. Remember to thoroughly examine the evidence you give to demonstrate your ability to think carefully and objectively.

Sources such as the National Institute for Health and Care Excellence (NICE) (2023) and Scottish Intercollegiate Guidelines Network (SIGN) (2023) are primary sources of evidence-based practice guidelines. NICE and SIGN provide comprehensive and extensively reviewed evidence-based recommendations in various areas. Use your university library to access academic journals and textbook databases–seek library support to refine your search techniques. Professional sources such as the RCN (2023a) and NMC (2022a) and government policies will be useful for your essay. Learning to reference accurately will help ensure that your marker can check the evidence you have utilised. Correctly citing your sources allows you to show what you have based the discussion upon and safeguards you from potential plagiarism accusations. Familiarise yourself with your university's referencing style, whether it is APA, MLA, Harvard, or another (Pears and Shields, 2022). Remember that consistency in referencing style is essential throughout your essays.

Establishing a clear and consistent file name system can help you track the progress of your essay. It can help prevent you from losing work or submitting the wrong version for marking. One approach is to put the version number or date in the file name as you proceed through drafts: for example, 'EssayTopic_V1' for the first draft, 'EssayTopic_V2' for the second, and so on. Consider renaming the final version, 'EssayTopic_Final', once finished. Keeping all your drafts in one folder might help you keep organised even more, but always keep backup copies in case you lose access. Consider using cloud storage services such as Google Drive or Dropbox, which include version history features. Sometimes your university may have a file naming convention you will need to use, so you may need to save a final version using the file name style required for submission. Before clicking the 'upload' button, always open and quickly inspect the file to ensure it is the correct version. Few assessment experiences are worse than losing your work or submitting an early draft instead of your final version.

Have your essay ready for upload at least a day before the deadline.

This step will enable you to deal with technical difficulties or problems during submission. There can be many issues that arise which can delay your upload, from file types to network issues. Having a buffer of at least a day can help you get support to resolve any difficulties and still submit your work before the deadline. It will reduce your stress levels and help to ensure you submit on time. If you want to write a good nursing essay, you must understand the assessment criteria well, write and edit it carefully, use evidence effectively and submit it on time. It is a time-consuming process, but practice and commitment will pay off. Another form of assessment you will likely encounter is group work.

Tips for group work

Group work assessments are essential to the university curriculum because they promote collaboration, communication, and shared learning. These tasks provide an opportunity to practice the type of teamwork that will be encountered in your professional life. They can, however, present difficulties, such as conflict, resolving differences and maintaining communication (Wong, Kan and Chow, 2022). Therefore, establishing clear communication channels from the start is vital. Determine how you will keep in touch through email, group chats, or frequent meetings. An open and polite approach can significantly benefit understanding each other's perspectives and thoughts, resulting in better outcomes and less chance for misunderstanding. After establishing good communication, divide roles and responsibilities among group members. This split should ideally be based on each member's unique skills and interests. Everyone needs to be involved during this crucial stage as this will promote inclusion and help to ensure agreement on how the group work will be completed. Remember that some group members may thrive at research, while others may excel at coordinating efforts or writing the report. Try to find out each person's strengths when designating group activities. It is essential to record each member's agreed tasks and deadlines carefully. These notes can then be referred to, keeping the project on track and helping to resolve any difficulties.

Activity 5.2: Group work style

This activity is intended to help you determine the type of contributor you often become during group work. This exercise is not about categorising yourself into a specific role. Instead, it is designed to help you recognise how you typically contribute to group work and how you can grow. Recognising your work style is an essential step towards effective collaboration, as it can help you build on your strengths and work on areas for development.

Reflect upon your previous experiences with group work, whether in your nursing education or previous work and education. Team projects and group presentations are examples. Think about the role you tend to play in these group settings. Are you often the one who starts conversations and leads the project? Are you the person who makes sure that different people's ideas are heard and considered? Or do you feel most comfortable coordinating tasks and keeping the group on track? Perhaps you are often the team member who contributes creativity and innovation or always offer support and encouragement when difficulties arise. It may be that you take on several roles or change depending upon the group or task, as this is commonly the case. List your observations and note any examples that come to mind. Consider how the role you have noted affects the group's functioning and dynamics. What skills do you bring, and are there any areas you need to work on? How do you feel about your role in group projects – is there a role you would like to adopt in future work? These insights can support your future contribution and growth, enhancing your ability to be an effective healthcare team member.

Questions

- *Can you recall a time when you needed to adapt or change your role in a group? What prompted this shift, and how did you deal with it?*
- *How does your knowledge of your group work style influence how you approach future teamwork situations?*

A suggested answer is given at the end of the chapter.

Plan for periodic discussions during group work projects to allow for review of progress and adjustments as needed. This approach not only helps to increase quality but will also help the project move forward as anticipated. Conflicts may arise in any cooperative project, especially one that is assessed (Polyakova-Norwood et al., 2023). It is essential to realise that these are not barriers to learning and progress but possibilities for learning and growth. When problems or disagreements develop, deal with them quickly and respectfully. Encourage open discussion about the issue, listen to all points of view, and work to find a solution that everyone can agree on. During these conversations, it is essential to avoid personal attacks and focus on the topic at hand. Dealing with a member not pulling their weight during group work can be difficult. In such cases, handling the problem within the group is often best. Gently remind the person of their obligations and refer to the tasks they agreed to complete. If the problem persists, you may need to contact your lecturer and provide them with details about the situation.

Your projects' success will depend upon efficient communication, clear roles and duties, regular quality checks, and constructive disagreement resolution. Each component will promote participation, respect, and cohesion among group members. Remember that group work will refine the teamwork and collaboration skills essential for providing high-quality patient care in pressurised nursing environments.

Feedback

Constructive feedback is an essential tool for improvement. Try to embrace it, whether from your practice supervisors, lecturers, classmates, or self-reflection. Some of the most potent feedback may come from patients, service users and family members (Morley, Bettles and Derham, 2019). Although many people can feel discomfort when receiving direct feedback, positive and critical feedback can significantly improve your skills and guide your learning journey. Engaging with feedback is one of the most vital aspects of the learning process for student nurses. Viewing feedback as a stepping-stone towards improvement rather than a critique of your abilities is essential. Being open to feedback will show those supporting your development that they can share their expert guidance and advice. Always consider asking for feedback on your performance during a specific task or procedure. Remember, feedback is not about personal shortcomings but about identifying professional opportunities for growth. Positive feedback is equally important to engage with, as it reinforces what you are doing well and should continue to do. Reviewing positive feedback can boost confidence and foster motivation (Sultan and Victor, 2021). When you receive feedback, actively engage with it by identifying key areas to take forward. Reflect on these points: what can you learn from them? How can you incorporate this feedback into your future work? Actively engaging with feedback means not just reading it and setting it aside but making a conscious effort to understand and apply it.

If specific points in the feedback are unclear, it is essential to seek clarification. It is better to ask for further explanation than to make assumptions that might not be correct. Your practice supervisors and lecturers are there to help you learn and will gladly offer additional guidance if asked. Using feedback to improve future work is arguably the most impactful way to engage with it. This can be achieved by creating an action plan based on your feedback. Identify the areas you need to work on, outline steps to address these areas, and monitor your progress over time. Implementing this feedback into your subsequent work will enhance your performance and demonstrate that you are proactive and dedicated to continuous learning. By engaging with feedback, you will set the stage for constant growth and development, attributes that are essential in the fast-evolving nursing profession.

Managing workload

Meeting your academic obligations, clinical placements, personal life, work, and self-care can feel like a juggling act. However, by striking a balance, you will be better able to manage stress, stay productive, and enjoy your university experience. The following tips will help you develop your time management skills:

- **Make a To-Do List or a Schedule**: Organise your assignments, exams, shifts, and other commitments. A visual representation of your time can help you see how it is being spent and where changes should be made. Many tools and apps are available to assist with this, such as Google Calendar, Microsoft Outlook, to-do apps, and traditional paper planners.
- **Prioritise your work:** Recognise that not all tasks are equal in importance. There are several techniques that you can use

to categorise tasks. This can assist you in determining what requires immediate attention and what can wait. Many productivity tools will enable you to prioritise tasks.

- **Take Regular Breaks:** It may seem counterintuitive, but regular short breaks can increase productivity and creativity (Septiani, 2022). A popular method is the Pomodoro Technique, which involves working for 25 minutes and then taking a five-minute break.
- **Avoid Multitasking:** While it may appear to be a good idea, attempting multiple tasks simultaneously can lead to a decrease in task errors and lower productivity (Lepp et al., 2019; Kononova and Yuan, 2017). It can be more effective to concentrate on one at a time.
- **Break down large tasks.** Large tasks can appear overwhelming, but breaking them into smaller, manageable tasks can make them less intimidating and more approachable. This method can assist you in making steady progress without becoming overwhelmed. Some student nurses find that mind mapping can help them visualise and break down large tasks (Ordu and Caliskan, 2023).
- **Maximise the time available:** Use the time between classes or commutes to complete smaller tasks such as reading an article, revising notes, or organising your calendar. This approach is known as "time chunking," and it can assist you in making the most of your available time.

- **Set Specific Goals:** Specific, attainable goals can help you stay motivated and focused. SMART (specific, measurable, achievable, relevant, and time-bound) can support your development in theory and practice (Manderscheid, 2022).
- **Seek Help When Needed:** As discussed in the self-care section later in this chapter, it is essential that if you are feeling overwhelmed, seek advice and assistance from your personal tutor or student support services. It is often best to do so earlier rather than later.

By implementing these strategies, you can manage your time more effectively while reducing stress and improving academic performance. Time management is a lifelong skill that will benefit your nursing career.

Dealing with Procrastination

Procrastination is the act of delaying or postponing tasks despite knowing that the consequences will be negative and is usually accompanied by feelings of anxiety (Badri Gargari, Sabouri and Norzad, 2011). Procrastination can cause stress, guilt, decreased productivity, and dissatisfaction with oneself and is a common stumbling block for many student nurses (Attia and Abdelwahid, 2020). Procrastination is not just a stumbling block; it can impede academic success in a demanding field like nursing. Recognising when you succumb to procrastination is the critical first step in combating it. Are you spending more time on social media than on your assignment? Do you frequently put off tasks that you perceive as difficult or monotonous? Identifying these patterns is critical for dealing with procrastination head-on. To overcome procrastination, one must first understand the 'why' of procrastination. Is the task too boring or too difficult? Are you disorganised or concerned that pursuing perfection will lead to failure? Recognising these elements can help you develop tailored strategies to combat procrastination. Additionally, the distractions must be identified and minimised. This could include turning off phone notifications, using apps that block access to distracting websites, or creating a calm, clutter-free workspace.

Scenario: Jac

Jac is an 18-year-old student nurse halfway through her first year of nursing studies. She is surprised at how quickly time has passed. Jac's known for her diligent and conscientious approach to her studies at school and, since starting at university, often goes the extra mile to ensure she is well-prepared for exams and clinical placements. However, she has faced a new challenge with two end-of-term essays due within the same week. Despite knowing the importance of these essays and their influence on her grades, Jac simply cannot bring herself to start them. Her computer's white and currently blank screen seems to resist her efforts to get started. Like many students in a similar position before her, she busies herself with other tasks. These include rearranging her home study space and sorting the apps on her phone. No matter how hard she tries, she cannot seem to get started with the essays.

Jac shares her difficulties with one of her friends, Samita, who is not having the same problems. Samita invites Jac to study with her at the university library. Jac accepts the offer despite initial hesitations and packs her laptops and notes. Once at the library, the atmosphere helps her get in the mood to study. Being surrounded by other students focused on their work inspires her to get started. Samita has broken down the essay into smaller tasks, such as understanding the essay question, making an outline, and beginning the first draft. They agreed on a routine: forty-five minutes of work and a fifteen-minute break to relax and chat. This approach of work and rest periods helps to maintain their progress. Encouraged, Jac and Samita plan to study this way during the weeks leading up to the deadline for the essays. Jac gradually finds her assessments taking shape. The experience taught her a valuable lesson about tackling procrastination tasks and the power of shared motivation.

Questions

- *In what ways did Jac's structured routine of work and rest periods aid her essay management?*
- *How did a friend's encouragement affect Jac's motivation and assignment progress?*

A suggested answer is given at the end of the chapter.

Using the time management techniques discussed earlier in this chapter can help to increase productivity and avoid procrastination. A difficult task can feel like an insurmountable mountain, leading to avoidance. One effective strategy is to divide your tasks into smaller, more manageable chunks. This reduces the intimidation factor and makes getting started less daunting. Adopting a benefits-focused mindset can also aid in the prevention of procrastination. Rather than focusing on the required effort, consider the benefits and satisfaction resulting from task completion. This shift in perspective can provide the motivation to overcome procrastination and start progressing (Williams, 2020).

Furthermore, remember that your physical and mental health significantly affects your procrastination. Regular physical activity, a well-balanced diet, and adequate sleep can increase your energy and concentration, lowering your chances of procrastination. We will consider these areas in more detail in the next section. If chronic procrastination persists, seek professional assistance. Academic advisors at your university should be able to help you understand the underlying causes of your procrastination and offer strategies for dealing with it. Remember that overcoming procrastination is a gradual process. There may be setbacks here and there, but the key is to keep trying new things until you find what works best for you. Controlling procrastination can boost productivity and help to reduce stress.

Social media use

The digital age has blurred the lines between professional and personal life, and managing the boundary between these two spheres can be difficult for student nurses. While social media can be an excellent tool for student nurses to network and identify professional development resources, it must be used cautiously (Alharbi, Kuhn and Morphet, 2020). Social media platforms can connect you with experienced nurses, allow you to participate in online forums, and give you access to educational materials. You can converse with other students and professionals to gain insights, share ideas, and feel a part of a larger community. It is a space to learn about the most recent research, clinical innovation, and best practice. The NMC (2022b) emphasises the importance of student nurses maintaining professional boundaries and confidentiality. Sharing information about patients, colleagues, or your workplace is strictly forbidden. Protecting a patient's privacy and dignity is critical, and failing to do so can result in serious professional consequences. Irresponsible use of social media may result in breaches of your university's student code of conduct and fitness to practice hearings.

Activity 5.3: Social media and patients

Consider a hypothetical situation in which the relative of a patient you are currently treating in placement attempts to connect with you on a social media platform, such as Facebook or Instagram. They ask you to share information about their loved one's health condition and treatment. How would you handle such a situation while adhering to professional standards? Create a script that describes how you would respond to this patient respectfully, professionally, and ethically. Your response should clearly communicate your boundaries, direct them to the appropriate channels for their inquiry, and respect the person's dignity. It may be beneficial to write responses to a variety of potential scenarios. Share your scenarios with a practice supervisor or peer to develop your understanding; they may have encountered similar situations. This activity should provide you with a better understanding of the importance of setting online boundaries as well as some practical tools for dealing with these situations when they arise. Professionally navigating social media can be a learning process, but its responsible use can bring benefits.

Questions

- *What further strategies could be implemented if a patient's relative was to continue crossing online boundaries despite your initial response?*
- *How might different social media platforms require different approaches to boundary setting?*

A suggested answer is given at the end of the chapter.

Your online behaviour must reflect the nursing profession's values and responsibilities. Derogatory remarks, unprofessional conduct, or inappropriate content could tarnish your reputation, that of the university and even the entire profession. It is always a good idea to seek advice from your university if you are unsure about the appropriate use of social media or encounter a situation where its use may be a professional concern.

Self-care

Entering the field of nursing can be an enriching but challenging experience. Study demands, clinical placements and the emotional intensity accompanying patient care can sometimes be overwhelming. Self-care must be an essential aspect of your student life, assisting you in maintaining your physical, mental, and emotional health as you progress through your studies. This section will explore approaches you can use to develop mindfulness, set boundaries, and maintain your physical health. Before we do so, one of the most important things you can do is to be kind to yourself. Remember that there will be ups and downs throughout the course. Do not be too hard on yourself if there are bumps along the way, and be sure to celebrate your accomplishments, no matter how minor they may appear. Recognising your achievements can boost motivation and remind you why you chose this path in the first place.

Setting boundaries

Setting and maintaining boundaries is essential in your professional and personal life, especially as a student nurse. Understanding how to set limits will help maintain balance and prevent burnout as you navigate the demands of rigorous academic coursework, clinical placements, and personal responsibilities. Remember that setting boundaries does not imply being selfish or unkind. View it as an essential aspect of self-preservation and ensuring you can commit to your duties without negatively impacting your well-being.

Due to factors associated with high workload and other factors, nurses can be at increased risk of fatigue, stress, or burnout (Boamah, Read and Spence Boamah, 2017). When it comes to physical, emotional, and mental capacities, everyone has different thresholds. Consider which activities drain you and which ones energise you. This insight can be a helpful guide in defining your boundaries. Be sensitive to how you feel and look for signs indicating that you have reached your limit and need a break. Burnout can include physical and psychological factors, such as reduced energy, feelings of hopelessness, depersonalisation, and various physical symptoms (Mudallal, Othman and Al Hassan, 2017). To help manage your well-being, setting boundaries is equally important in your clinical placements. Expectations about your availability for work and volunteering on top of your studies may need to be managed (see the concept box). While these experiences can be rewarding and educational, they should not come at the expense of your physical or mental health.

Sometimes simple steps such as telling friends or family that you need a quiet night can make a difference and help you keep in control. While socialising is essential, you need to find a balance that works for you. Remember that not everyone has to work a long shift in a clinical placement early the following day! So, be assertive and direct while remaining considerate in your communication (Razik et al., 2021). When you express your needs and responsibilities as a student nurse, most people will be understanding and supportive. Another crucial area is maintaining professional boundaries in patient interactions (Thomson, Smith and Karpa, 2023). As a student nurse, you may encounter intense and emotionally charged situations. Providing compassionate care without bringing the weight of each patient's experience home is critical. Developing strategies for 'switching off' from placement and decompressing can help to maintain these emotional boundaries. These may include techniques such as mindfulness and meditation, as discussed below. Additionally, speak to your practice supervisor or personal tutor for advice on managing and maintaining professional boundaries.

Concept box: Saying no

Saying no to work and other demands from others can be a huge issue that can be difficult for many student nurses who often put others before themselves. You may have requests from many different sources while studying, such as your family, friends, peers, employer, placements, and university lecturers. While you may want to agree to every request, this may not be realistic without holding back your progress. Therefore, you must know your limits and not overcommit yourself. As a nursing student, you may feel obligated to take on more than you can handle, whether an extra shift, another project, or a social commitment. Learning to prioritise your well-being is critical, so have an honest discussion with those in your life about the challenges that being a nursing student brings. Be prepared to say no to requests that may jeopardise your studies or lead to you being overwhelmed.

Setting boundaries is a continuous process. As circumstances change, you may need to reassess and adjust your limits. Self-reflection on a regular basis will be essential in this process, and remember that it is okay to seek assistance if you are having difficulty establishing or maintaining your boundaries.

Mindfulness and meditation

Mindfulness and meditation can be practical self-care tools. These practices can reduce stress, improve concentration, and promote peace and balance. Even a few minutes of quiet reflection or deep breathing daily can make a big difference. Though closely related, the concepts of mindfulness and meditation offer distinct paths to improved mental well-being, stress reduction, and an overall sense of inner calm.

Mindfulness is the practice of fully immersing in the present moment. It can assist us to live in the 'here and now,' allowing our worries to be put aside. The practice can positively affect student nurses' emotional intelligence and communication skills (Snowden et al., 2015; Sundling, 2017). Mindfulness enables us to observe our thoughts, feelings, and sensations without judgement, noting them and allowing them to pass without dominating our consciousness. It can begin with simple activities. For example, consider the flavours, textures, and aromas when eating a meal. Concentrate on the sensation of your feet touching the ground, the wind against your skin, and the sounds around you while walking. It is about quieting the mind's constant chatter and more fully engaging with the world around you. You can incorporate mindfulness into your nursing studies as well. When reading or writing, try to concentrate solely on that activity. If your mind wanders to other thoughts or concerns, gently bring it back to the task. Approaches such as these can assist with developing confidence and belief in your writing skills (Drewery, Westlund Stewart and Wilson, 2022). Additionally, mindful studying can boost concentration and information retention, making your sessions more productive.

Meditation is a more formal practice in which you make time to quiet your mind and cultivate inner peace. There are many different types of meditation, but one of the most basic involves focused breathing exercises. Close your eyes and concentrate solely on your breath - the sensation of air entering and leaving your body. If thoughts arise, acknowledge them before letting them go and returning your attention to your breath. Meditation regularly has been shown to reduce stress and anxiety among nursing students (Heinrich and O'Connell, 2023). It can also improve healthcare professionals' focus and concentration, positively influencing their sleep (van der Riet, Levett-Jones and Aquino-Russell, 2018). Neuroimaging techniques have shown meditation to cause changes in brain areas associated with attention, emotion regulation, and self-awareness (Nakamura et al., 2021; Guendelman, Medeiros and Rampes, 2017). It can provide a sense of balance and calm, which is especially useful while seeking to relax before and after time in your practice placement.

Incorporating mindfulness and meditation into your daily routine does not require significant changes. It can begin with a few minutes daily and gradually increase as you find what works best. The more practice, the more influential the benefits of improved mental well-being and resilience will help you with your studies. The RCN (2019) has developed resources to help you practise mindfulness in a section on their website called 'Time and Space'. We have included details in the useful websites section of this chapter.

Physical health

One of the main foundations of self-care is good physical health. As a student nurse, you must get sufficient sleep, eat a balanced diet, and exercise regularly. Amid all the demands of studying nursing, these things may appear simple and inconsequential. However, they significantly impact your progress and ability to succeed by affecting your energy levels, mood, cognitive functioning, and overall health.

The value of a well-balanced and nutritious diet cannot be overstated. With hectic schedules, lack of food options, and irregular hours, nurses can often find little time for healthy eating (Keogh, 2014). This fact does not remove the importance of providing your body with the proper nutrients, including fruits, vegetables, lean proteins, and whole grains. These will help to boost your energy, immune function, and overall health. Try to find ways of preparing meals in advance so that they are still available even when you are busy. Maintaining hydration is also essential and has been shown to help to avoid impairment in cognitive function among healthcare professionals (El-Sharkawy et al., 2016). Drink plenty of water throughout the day, especially during long shifts or study sessions, to stay hydrated.

Student Insights

"I've gotten into a routine where I've picked set days to go to the gym and worked it around my university timetable, I'm taking my own lunch to university. So I think it'll be more achievable now that I'm organised"

Student nurse research participant

(Smith, Disler Watson, 2020, p.539)

Another pillar of physical health is maintaining adequate levels of activity. Regular exercise has numerous advantages for nursing students, including improved cardiovascular health, mood, sleep, and stress reduction (Wirth et al., 2023). This does not imply that you must train for a marathon or spend hours at the gym daily. Find an activity you enjoy, such as yoga, dancing, hiking, or simply walking briskly. Even short, regular breaks to stretch or go for a quick walk can be beneficial, particularly during long study periods or shifts. Linked to physical activity is sleep. It can be easy to sacrifice sleep for late-night study sessions or early morning shifts, but not getting enough sleep can have a negative impact on your health, cognitive function, and risk of errors while in practice (Kotera et al., 2021). Try to stick to a consistent sleep schedule, aiming for 7-9 hours of sleep per night where possible. Limiting screen time before bed, keeping your sleep environment dark and quiet, and avoiding caffeine and large meals close to bedtime can all help improve your sleep quality (Irish et al., 2015).

Additionally, regular medical check-ups are essential for maintaining physical health. Ensure you do not forget to attend regular dental and eye exams while studying and seek medical attention early if you have any health problems. As a student nurse, you will likely become excellent at caring for others but do not forget to care for yourself.

Conclusion

In conclusion, this chapter has considered how to succeed by managing your well-being to excel during your studies. We have set out essential NMC requirements to help you understand how to progress effectively. There are also tips on how to pass your assessments and remember to use the resources at the end of this chapter to develop your study skills further. You will need to effectively manage your workload to achieve the requirements of your nursing studies. It will enable you to prioritise, organise, and distribute your tasks to fit your schedule and personal needs. In addition, planning and awareness are needed to overcome procrastination. Nursing is widely recognised as a demanding profession, which brings with it a requirement for self-care. Busy student nurses often neglect areas such as mindfulness and maintaining boundaries. However, these aspects of your well-being can reduce stress and provide time and energy for rest and rejuvenation. Becoming a skilled nurse requires you to look after yourself, as this will enable you to look after others.

Suggested answers

Activity 5.1

Unpacking an essay question is a process that can easily be applied to other types of assessments. The first step in any project proposal, case study, exam question, or presentation is always to understand what is being asked of you. You can apply this approach to virtually any academic task by identifying key terms and expectations, breaking complex tasks into manageable parts, and formulating an initial plan or response. This method promotes a thorough understanding of the assignment, allowing you to approach your work more flexibly and strategically.

After completing this activity, you may approach essay questions in the future with a more methodical and analytical mindset. Instead of jumping right into research or writing, you would probably spend more time first understanding and interpreting the question. This could include identifying keywords, breaking down the question into smaller components, and brainstorming a brief action plan based on your understanding. This more deliberate and thorough approach may improve your essays' quality while making the process more efficient and less stressful.

Activity 5.2

When recalling a time when you adapted or changed your role within a group, you may have thought about a project where one team member struggled with their part of the work. Although you often find yourself in the role of coordinator, ensuring that tasks are completed on time, you found yourself in a more supportive role in this instance. You took the time to talk the other team member through the project, explaining concepts and providing resources to support them. An example such as this shows the value of versatility in group work, demonstrating that you sometimes need to step outside your typical role to ensure the team's overall success.

Understanding your group work style can help you approach future teamwork situations more effectively. For example, if you recognise that you tend to take on leadership roles, you might also consider consciously creating space for others to lead. You may do so to encourage a more collaborative environment. Alternatively, if you frequently play a supportive role, you could challenge yourself to take on more decision-making responsibilities to develop your leadership skills. Recognising your preferred style also assists you in identifying your strengths and weaknesses, enabling you to concentrate on improving your solid points and developing areas that would benefit from improvement. Understanding your group work style can assist with ongoing personal and professional development.

Scenario Jac

Jac's structured routine of working for 45 minutes and taking a 15-minute break, a variation on the Pomodoro Technique, helped her essay management. It established a consistent work rhythm that allowed her to concentrate and make progress on her essays during work intervals. At the same time, regular breaks prevented her from getting too tired while keeping her motivated. This work-rest balance helped to make the daunting task of writing two essays more manageable. Furthermore, the regular breaks allowed her to return to her assignment with fresh eyes, likely improving the quality of her work.

Jac's motivation and progress were greatly influenced by having her friend alongside her during the essay-writing process. The mutual commitment to a shared study schedule brought a level of accountability to her friend, making it more difficult for Jac to procrastinate. Samita's encouragement and advice created a supportive environment that made completing the essays seem more manageable. The shared experience of working together and taking breaks adds a social component to an isolating situation. These factors increased Jac's motivation and helped her progress with her essays.

Activity 5.3

You have several options if a patient's relative continues to cross online boundaries despite your initial response. You can reiterate your boundaries to remind them, politely but firmly, of professional considerations. Escalate the situation to a higher level by notifying your university and practice supervisor. They will be able to offer advice and support and intervene on your behalf if necessary. The use of platform features may be appropriate in some circumstances. Most social media platforms allow you to block or restrict specific users. If the situation demands it and the person persists, these features may be used as a last resort.

Because different social media platforms have varying levels of personal and professional interaction, varied approaches to boundary setting may be required. Each platform has its privacy settings that should be used to help keep these boundaries in place. However, the NMC (2022b) emphasises that even the strictest privacy settings have limitations, and once something is online, it can be copied and redistributed. Understanding the nature and features of each platform can aid in developing an appropriate online professional presence.

Recommended reading

Essential Study Skills: The Complete Guide to University Success by Tom Burns and Sandra Sinfield (2022) is a practical guide intended to assist students at all levels in improving their study skills.

Mindfulness for Students, also by Stella Cottrell (2018), shows you how mindfulness can be applied to your studies and everyday life. It takes you through tools and techniques for different study contexts, such as listening to lectures, completing assignments, and preparing for exams.

The Study Skills Handbook by Stella Cottrell (2019) is a comprehensive guide to help you develop the skills needed to improve performance within your university studies. While it is not specifically for student nurses, the principles apply to students across disciplines.

Useful websites

The ***RCN*** (2019) has carried out a project called 'Time and Space' to make mindfulness accessible to all RCN members. It gives nurses simple exercises to connect to their senses, breathe mindfully, and notice their emotions and thoughts throughout the day. ***https://www.rcn.org.uk/healthy-workplace/healthy-you/time-and-space***

Sage Study Skills offers information and a selection of free resources to help students improve their academic performance. The page provides free resources linked to Sage books which are available to buy if desired, such as ebooks, quizzes, and webinars. ***https://uk.sagepub.com/en-gb/eur/study-skills***

To help students transition to higher education, ***UCAS*** offers a range of helpful study skills guides. You can learn practical, independent study habits from the guides' activities and advice. Guides on time management, proofreading and editing, academic essay writing, and presenting an argument are available. ***https://www.ucas.com/undergraduate/student-life/study-skills-guides***

University of Oxford's (2023) guide to essay and dissertation writing skills is packed with helpful information and tips. It covers the main features of essay structure, such as the introduction, main body, conclusion, and references. It also advises on interpreting essay questions, planning and structuring your writing, and citing sources. ***https://www.ox.ac.uk/students/academic/guidance/skills/essay***

THRIVING DURING YOUR STUDIES

Introduction

Once you have started to settle into your course, you will begin to develop an understanding of how the university system operates. In this chapter, we will assist you in making the most of the information, resources and guidance required to thrive during your studies. We will explain the role of the personal tutor and student support services. The personal tutor, an essential figure in your academic journey, provides support and is often responsible for monitoring your progress and checking you have met specific professional requirements. The library is an essential resource that you can access alongside academic services to progress your study skills rapidly. We will explain the various services that are typically available and provide tips on how to use them to enhance your learning and performance. This chapter will provide the information you need to navigate your course confidently.

Personal Tutor

Many universities have personal tutors, sometimes called personal advisors or similar, who will be an essential source of support during your nursing studies. You will usually be allocated a lecturer who will serve as your first point of contact if you have any concerns or difficulties. They can help you with everything from course content to providing pastoral care, including advice and help accessing further assistance if you have any problems. Your personal tutor is an academic staff member who may or may not teach your course (Walker, 2022). Their responsibilities usually include supporting your transition into university and between levels, discussing academic progress and being an initial point of contact if you require support. University life can be difficult sometimes, and your personal tutor can help you navigate any personal, emotional, or health issues that may arise during your studies. They may also be role models to support student development (White et al., 2018). They will also

> ***Student insights***
>
> *"I believe I would not have overcome difficulties and carried on with the course to the point I am now if it was not for my personal tutor."*
>
> *Student nurse research participant*
>
> *(Braine and Parnell, 2011, p.908)*

provide support and signpost you to relevant university support services so you can get further assistance.

In nurse education, your personal tutor will often be a registered nurse in the same field of practice as you. The position is often combined with the NMC (2018b) role of academic assessor, who liaises with your practice assessor from placements to monitor and verify your progress. However, you cannot have the same academic assessor for all the years of the nursing programme, so you may find either your personal tutor changes at some point or the two roles are split between different people. Additionally, they can change if the lecturer changes position or leaves the university. If you experience any difficulties and concerns during your studies, always consider contacting your personal tutor as early as possible. They will be able to provide practical support and guidance. Remember, their goal is to assist you in succeeding in your nurse education.

Student support

Universities recognise the variety of challenges students may encounter and provide a range of student services. Financial advice, housing services, disability services, international student support, and career counselling are examples of such services (UCAS, 2023f). In recognition of the pressures that university can place on students, particularly those studying intensive programmes like nursing, counselling and mental health support are often available. These services provide professional and confidential assistance with issues you may be experiencing. Face-to-face and online support is usually available, so check the university website or speak with a student support advisor. Your personal tutor will point you in the right direction as necessary. Another source of support is your Student Union or Student Association. It represents the student body, defending your rights and helps to ensure the student's voice is heard within the university. You can also get involved with the National Union of Students (2023), which aims to achieve national change for students. They also plan social events, include clubs and societies, and provide advice.

Disability Services

University disability services support students with additional needs or abilities, such as physical and mental health conditions, sensory impairments, and neurodiversity. Neurodiversity refers to recognising and celebrating differences in the human brain and how people think, learn, and process information (Pearce, 2022). Accepting neurodiversity means accepting that these differences are natural and valuable aspects of human diversity rather than flaws that must be fixed. Disability services help to ensure an inclusive and accessible environment for all students. Nursing students may require specific support and accommodations to ensure they can progress through their studies. This may include assistance and accommodations to students with specialised equipment and individualised reasonable adjustments for learning and assessment.

For example, a nursing student with a hearing impairment may require an amplified stethoscope or one built for use with hearing aids. Disability services are available for students who develop a disability or chronic health condition while at university and those whose disability status changes. You can access the service even if you do not have a formal diagnosis, and advisors will often be able to provide advice regarding how to undergo assessment for a suspected condition. Various pieces of legislation underpin these approaches, including the Equality Act (2010). It safeguards the rights of applicants and students with a disability. The legislation prohibits disability discrimination, harassment, and victimisation and requires universities to make reasonable accommodations for disabled students. Disability services will sometimes contribute to university-wide approaches to ensure inclusive teaching and learning, ensuring that university systems meet the needs of neurodiverse students.

Scenario: Hadiza

Hadiza is a 33-year-old first-year nursing student studying to become a learning disability nurse. She has always been a hardworking and determined person. Hadiza was enthusiastic about her studies and committed to her future career. During the programme's early stages, she struggled with certain aspects of her coursework that she could not quite grasp. Engaging with reading required in advance of classes took longer than expected, and she frequently had to reread passages several times to understand them fully. Written assignments, such as essays, became a huge source of frustration as she struggled to organise her thoughts and express them clearly on paper. Hadiza got to the point where she realised that she needed some support. She approached her personal tutor and shared her difficulties, noting that a few issues were identified at school but had never been formally assessed. Given Hadiza's concerns, the personal tutor suggested she contact the university's student support services for further guidance.

Following her tutor's advice, Hadiza contacted student support services and expressed her concerns. The staff listened to her carefully and scheduled an assessment to review her learning needs. The evaluation was in-depth, exploring various aspects of Hadiza's learning processes. It felt good for Hadiza to open up about her problems with someone who understood. When the assessment results came in, they confirmed what Hadiza had suspected for a long time: she had a form of dyslexia. Rather than being disheartened by the diagnosis, Hadiza felt relieved as she finally had an explanation for the difficulties she had been experiencing. The diagnosis meant she was entitled to more support from the university, including more time for assessments, which relieved some of her stress. She learned about strategies and tools that could help manage her academic work and clinical placements, such as how to organise her thoughts. Hadiza gradually saw improvements in her studies and placements.

Question

- *What can we learn from Hadiza's story about recognizing and addressing learning differences in educational and professional settings?*

A suggested answer is given at the end of the chapter.

Disability services support the coordination and provision of reasonable adjustments to ensure students with a disability have equal access to learning opportunities (Sheerin and Curtis, 2019). Extra time for exams, note-taking services, assistive technology, alternative formats for course materials, and changes in clinical placement settings are all examples of this. These measures can significantly affect a student nurse's ability to participate fully in their studies. Additionally, disability services promote an inclusive university environment and guide staff to help them meet the needs of a diverse student population (Lopez-Gavira, Moriña, and Morgado, 2021). They will often support students to help them manage their disabilities while at university, including stress management techniques and strategies for navigating the physical environment of the university and placement settings. They will also guide with academic skills, such as time management techniques specific to a particular condition. Another central role of many disability services is advocacy. Advisers may advocate for students with lecturers and other university departments to ensure their needs are understood and met. They will collaborate with other student services such as funding, student support and academic advising.

If you have a disability, accessing support as early as possible is essential. You can often begin this while still an applicant or shortly after starting the programme. The first step is finding more information via the university website or visiting student services. You can meet with a coordinator or assessor who will discuss your needs with you and arrange further assessments if required. Disability Services can be very busy during the first few weeks of the term when many new students are starting, so make arrangements as early as possible. As a healthcare student, you will likely have an occupational health review around the start of your studies, and you should highlight if you have a disability during the appointment, as appropriate. The occupational health specialist may be able to guide the university regarding your needs and any reasonable adjustments that are required (NHS Employers, 2021). Disability services may share necessary information with lecturers, although discussing your needs with your personal tutor can also be helpful. Remember to keep disability services updated if your circumstances or needs change.

Financial and funding services

Financial advisors are commonly available via student services and can help you manage your budget, understand tuition fees, and even apply for scholarships or grants. For a detailed description of nursing students' funding options, please see Chapter 3.

Counselling and mental health services:

As mentioned earlier, universities understand students' stresses, particularly those pursuing demanding programmes such as nursing.

Mental health needs among students, including nursing students, have risen in recent years (Office for National Statistics, 2021; UK Parliament, 2023). They provide counselling services where you can talk about any problems you have with issues such as stress, anxiety, and depression (Vescovelli et al., 2017). Consider speaking with your personal tutor, who can point you in the right direction or speak directly with student services. Many universities also provide access to online resources to support your well-being and mental health (Abu Shahim et al., 2021). These services may complement support you are receiving from other sources, such as your GP. Specific support may also be available if you are in distress and need urgent assistance, including out-of-hours services. The university website will usually provide details on accessing support in this situation. In these circumstances, you should also consider accessing professional assistance, including emergency NHS services if necessary.

Activity 6.1: Mental health online support

Maintaining your mental well-being while studying can be challenging at times. As a student nurse, you must learn how to care for your patient's mental health as well as your own. This activity is intended to assist you in exploring online mental health resources that may be useful if you need additional support at any stage during your studies. Of course, your university will often be the first source of mental health support, but it is also worth being aware of resources such as those below that may be helpful to students across the country.

To begin, choose <u>one</u> of the following online mental health organisations and visit their website:

***Student Minds** is a student mental health charity. They equip students and university community members to care for their mental health, support others, and effect change. Student Minds provides various resources, including information on the challenges that university life can bring.*

***Mind** is a mental health charity that provides information and support to people with mental health issues. They have a page dedicated to student mental health support and treatment and a list of organisations and charities that can assist.*

***Anxiety UK** is a charity that assists people diagnosed with anxiety disorder. They have a student membership and information about being a student affected by anxiety. They provide a helpline, which can be reached by dialling 03444 775 774, as well as a variety of resources and information on their website.*

***The Mental Health Foundation** is a charity providing information and support to people with mental health issues or learning disabilities. They provide various resources and information on their website, including those aimed at students, as well as a helpline that can be reached by dialling 0300 123 33934.*

Spend time exploring the resource you have chosen. Understand the platform's key features, such as its services and support. If the organisation is not specific to students, try typing the word 'student' into the search function on the website. Read through the information and guidance available to students. Take note of any support services that are provided. Consider the ease of use when navigating the resource and whether you think it would be helpful to a student nurse experiencing a mental health issue. Note why you chose this particular resource and how you believe it can help you as a student nurse's mental health. Finally, think about your mental health requirements and preferences and whether this may be a worthwhile resource to use now or in the future.

Question

- *How did exploring this online mental health resource increase your understanding of national resources available for mental health?*

A suggested answer is given at the end of the chapter.

IT services

TIT services ensure you have access to the technology you need for your studies, from Wi-Fi to software support. They ensure that the university's digital infrastructure runs smoothly at the most basic level. This includes the networks, servers, and databases that enable you to access online learning platforms and other resources. IT services will work with other departments, such as marketing, to manage the university's website and other student records so you can register, view your grades, pay tuition, and other essential things. They can also provide training in specific software you may need for your course. If you experience difficulties accessing a particular service or platform, reach out to IT, who can usually assist. This support can include help with problems with uploading assessments and saving your work, so remember they are there to help if you need assistance. IT departments will have a role in managing the Learning Management System (LMS) the university uses. The LMS provides online learning content and enables its management (Najmul Islam and Azad, 2015). Common examples are Moodle and Blackboard. You will become very familiar with the LMS during your studies as it will typically be used to host course materials, facilitate online discussions, assessment submissions, and other functions.

The university IT department usually offers a help desk where you can get help with any technological difficulties. They will help with Wi-Fi connections, computer problems and guidance on how to use the university systems. Another essential aspect of many university IT departments is ensuring students can access the software programs they need to study. These may include access to a word processing and presentation software suite, including Microsoft's (2023) popular Word and PowerPoint applications (see the concept box for more details). Other software platforms offering similar functions are provided through Google Docs and Apple's iWork suite. Before purchasing any licences, check what the university can offer. Students can often get discounts on the software they may use during their studies, so check with the provider before purchasing at the full price.

Concept box: Microsoft applications

Many universities now provide students with free access to Microsoft 365. This subscription-based platform includes access to Microsoft apps such as Teams, Word, Excel, PowerPoint, Outlook, and OneDrive. You may also get cloud storage to safely save your documents, resources, and assessments. One of the advantages of Microsoft 365 is that it allows you to work across different devices. You can then access your account and files on a university computer and then pick up where you left off at home. The university staff may use Microsoft's collaboration and videoconferencing software app called Teams to chat and meet online with you, although some use alternative platforms such as Zoom.

University campuses include computers you can use for your studies in computer labs or areas such as the library. IT services manage these; some may also provide laptop loan schemes, so check what is available. As mentioned in Chapter 3, you may be able to get assistance with purchasing a laptop through hardship funding if you meet specific criteria. Speak with student services for more information. Another vital role they play is through ensuring digital security. They put in place safeguards to protect the university's IT systems and the personal information of students and staff. They will provide information on protecting their devices and avoiding digital threats.

Career services

Career services can help you understand nursing students' various career paths and opportunities (Andrewartha and Harvey, 2017). These services offer career counselling, assistance with CVs and job applications, and the organisation of career fairs and networking events. They can be instrumental as you near graduation or when exploring your career options as you progress through the programme. As you will discover in Chapter 8, there are a wealth of different opportunities in nursing across hospital, community, and non-clinical settings. Career officers can provide insight into the options and may highlight opportunities you are unaware of. They may also help you with applying for jobs and how to write effective CVs and cover letters. The careers services will often provide strategies for successful interviews or direct you to relevant resources that will help. They may offer one-on-one career counselling so you can discuss your specific career goals, concerns, and challenges. This can all be useful when you start applying for roles as you approach the end of your nursing studies. Speak with Student Services if you are unsure how to access the careers service.

Academic skills

Academic skills services can assist you with academic writing, study skills, and even nursing-specific tutoring. They can help with essential skills such as essay writing, critical thinking, study strategies, and time management (Gamble et al., 2020). The academic services team will often run workshops, and there are usually opportunities to book group or one-to-one appointments. It is essential to book support from academic skills early, and many students will start taking up appointments and filling out workshops as deadlines approach. Do not leave it until a couple of weeks before submission, as you may find it hard to get support. Instead, access support early and always go prepared with questions you would like to ask or an extract of your writing. The advisors are experts in structuring and expressing your work in the best way possible. They will often be knowledgeable about the assessments in the nursing programme. However, they will not usually guide the nursing-specific aspects of your assignments – direct any queries about this content to the nurse lecturers.

Activity 6.2: Academic skills support

This activity is designed to help you gain a practical understanding of the academic skills support available at their university. It focuses on identifying a workshop relevant to your nursing studies. Begin by investigating what academic skills services your university provides. Often, this information is readily available on the university's website, through student portals, or in the student handbook. Take note of the services offered, paying attention to workshops or seminars focusing on academic skills that could be useful for your nursing studies. These skills might include essay writing, critical thinking, study strategies, presentation, and time management. Once you understand what is offered, identify a specific workshop or seminar that you believe may be useful. These often run throughout the year but are usually most commonly available during teaching periods. Perhaps you could identify a workshop on effective essay writing which would assist in writing your nursing essays or case studies. Or maybe there's a time management session to help juggle coursework, placements, and part-time work. Identify the aims that will be covered, the length of the session, who is delivering it, and any prerequisites or preparation required. You may even establish if the workshop's content applies to nursing studies. Once you have all the information, why not sign up for the workshop and commit to attending? Set a reminder in your calendar to ensure you do not forget. After attending the workshop, spend some time reflecting on your experience. Consider what you have learned and how this knowledge can be applied to your nursing studies.

Questions

- *What do you hope to gain from this workshop, and how will it affect your academic performance?*
- *Were you considering other workshops? What influenced your decision to attend the workshop?*

A suggested answer is given at the end of the chapter.

Academic skills can also help you develop effective note-taking techniques and improve reading and comprehension skills. These areas can include understanding and retaining the complex clinical and physiology information you will encounter as a student nurse. Time management and organisation are also vital for nursing students as the programme is demanding, and they often have other responsibilities outside their studies. An advisor can help you develop a study plan, balance coursework with placements and manage the workload. As discussed in Chapter 5, they can also help you deal with the common problem of procrastination. Often your course will require you to carry out presentations, and academic skills can provide guidance on constructing and delivering an effective presentation. The time you invest in developing these skills will benefit you both as a student nurse and throughout your career.

Library

The university library is an essential resource for nursing students to become familiar with. University libraries are more than just a place to borrow books; they are a hub of resources, services, and support that assist your academic progress. They promote the development of critical thinking, progressive thought, and information literacy (Green, 2020). The library has an extensive collection of physical and digital books, journals, and periodicals. As a nursing student, you will have access to a wealth of healthcare and nursing-specific literature, textbooks, and journals to supplement your coursework and research. Take time to familiarise yourself with the library and where the nursing resources are located. Often, you can take a real or virtual tour during the early stages of your programme. Alternatively, ask a librarian where the nursing and healthcare section can be found. Many resources are online, so building familiarity with the library website will be helpful.

Your library has access to various academic databases with research articles and scholarly content that will be vital for your essays and projects. There are specific databases for medical and nursing students, such as CINAHL, Medline and PubMed. The CINAHL (EBSCO, 2023) database is a good starting point as it is one of the most authoritative nursing and allied health databases. However, accessing various databases when searching for evidence is often worthwhile. Your university may have a search function that enables you to access multiple databases simultaneously. You will learn more about how to use these during your course, and if you see any workshops or sessions to become more knowledgeable about these databases, it will be well worth attending. Each hour spent learning how to use them effectively can improve your grades and save many frustrating hours in the long run!

Activity 6.3: Library

This activity aims to help you become familiar with your university's online library resources. To achieve this, we will focus on discovering a journal article and a book on the theme of 'patient-centred care.' Knowing how to use your online library resources effectively is essential in nursing education as it enables you to access reliable, evidence-based material that can inform your practice. Begin by visiting the library's website at your university. This is usually available on the main university website, or your course may provide a link directly. Once you have arrived at the library's homepage, become acquainted with its layout. Take note of where you can find various resources, such as books, articles, journals, and databases. There should be information available about how to search for sources. Now search for a journal article about 'patient-centred care.' You may need to use a database for this, although libraries often provide a unified search function incorporating multiple databases. If you wish to use a specific database CINAHL, PubMed, and MEDLINE are popular databases for nursing and healthcare literature. Enter the search term 'patient-centred care' into the database search engine and narrow your results using filters such as publication date. If your results are not specific enough, try adding the word 'nurse'.

Once you have found a suitable article, download it and make a note of the details. Next, look for a book on the same topic. Check the original search results. Do they include books as well as journal articles? If not, return to the main library search function and repeat the process checking that books are included in the results. Once you have found a suitable book, note whether it is available as an e-book or a physical copy and how you can obtain it. If you experience difficulties with searching for the items, seek support from a librarian. Conclude this activity by summarising your findings. Write a brief outline of the article and book, emphasising their relevance to patient-centred care. Consider whether the information is relevant to your studies and if the sources might help you prepare for one or more assessments.

Questions

- *How can the insights provided by the article and book inform your nursing practice?*

- *What further steps might be necessary if you cannot find the sources through the online library search?*

A suggested answer is given at the end of the chapter.

You will find that your library may have study spaces designed to accommodate different learning styles, such as silent study areas, group study rooms, and computer labs (Bryant, Matthews and Walton, 2009). Find a space that works for you, and then get into the habit of going there when you have free time between classes or at a time of the day that suits you. If studying from home, try to find a study space conducive to learning and use it in the same way. Librarians are a valuable and underutilised resource. They are not only there to help you find books, but they can also help you with your research by showing you how to use databases effectively, advising you on referencing styles, and assisting you in locating reliable sources for your assignments. Libraries typically have extended hours, with many providing 24-hour access during exam periods. Check your library's hours and take advantage of their availability. Remember that the library and its staff are there to help you succeed in your academic journey. When you require assistance or guidance, do not be afraid to ask for it.

Conclusion

To thrive during your studies, ensure that you access the wide range of support services available at university. You will start by learning about the university's course structure, theoretical and practical learning, self-directed study, and collaboration. Use student and academic support services to assist with your well-being, mental health, financial guidance, and academic advice. You will have a nominated member of the academic team, called a personal tutor or similar, who will provide pastoral care and support your professional development. The university library will help you with books, journals, online databases, and academic skill workshops. These resources will aid your research, assignments, and knowledge. Remember that thriving on your course requires more than passing assessments and completing placements. It involves using all the resources and expertise at your fingertips as an enrolled student at university.

Suggested answers

Scenario: Hadiza

Hadiza's story demonstrates the importance of recognising and addressing learning differences in educational and professional settings. By acknowledging her difficulties and seeking help, Hadiza gained access to resources supporting her learning. Her story demonstrates that learning differences, when correctly identified and accommodated, do not have to be a barrier to success. Hadiza's experience also highlights the importance of institutions responsive to diverse learning needs. The university played a central role in facilitating Hadiza's academic success through the support and guidance provided. Her story reminds us that there is no one-size-fits-all approach to learning. Every student has different learning needs, and recognising and accommodating these differences creates an inclusive learning environment where everyone can thrive.

Activity 6.1

You may have extended your understanding of national resources available for mental health. The sites all contained information specific to students and could be a valuable source of support depending on your needs. Remember that these will likely change throughout your studies. Many of these resources also provide information about mental health promotion and the benefits of prevention and early intervention rather than just crisis management. Having completed this activity, you may now wish to review the other websites in the list. These all have the potential to provide helpful information and support as you navigate the challenges of your nursing studies.

Activity 6.2

When selecting the workshop, you may have considered your current academic needs in the nursing course. If you choose essay writing, for example, you will likely gain skills that will help improve your academic writing skills. This workshop may offer strategies such as structuring essays, critically analysing sources, or improving grammar and punctuation. Improvements in these areas will improve the overall quality of your writing and the experience for those reading through your work. This will enhance your academic performance and, over time, your confidence in this academic skill.

You may have considered several options while determining the workshop. Perhaps workshops on academic referencing, presentation skills, or exam strategies were available. As a nursing student, you must engage in various forms of learning and assessment. Understanding why you chose the session may help you identify priority areas. Was there another workshop or session that appealed to you? While student nurses are often very busy, an hour or so spent learning about a specific academic skill can save significant amounts of time and effort in future. Remember that those delivering these sessions will have expertise and experience developing students' academic skills and will be able to guide you, so you do not have to figure it out yourself.

Activity 6.3

The knowledge gained from the article and book you chose may significantly improve your understanding of patient-centred care and how to apply it in your nursing practice. Peer-reviewed journal articles are credible and reliable sources that contain theoretical information and research findings that provide evidence for practice. Professional books are often written by an expert in the field and draw upon relevant evidence from many sources. The resources may cover topics related to patient-centred care, such as its principles, importance, and implementation in various health and social care settings. Understanding the theory behind patient-centred care can help you understand why it is a central approach within nursing practice. The resources chosen may provide practical examples and case studies demonstrating how patient-centred care works in real-world settings. These insights can help you develop strategies and approaches for your nursing practice. Journal articles and books on patient-centred care often address the challenges and obstacles that may arise and potential solutions. This will help you anticipate and prepare for these challenges in your practice, helping you provide care focused on the patient's needs, preferences, and values.

Often it can take some time and practice to search and find information efficiently. Expect a level of frustration, but it will get easier as you progress and become more familiar with the functions.

If you can not find the specific information you are looking for, try not to give up. First, reconsider your search strategy. Perhaps your search terms are too specific or too broad. Can you think of any other words to describe what you are looking for? Sometimes Boolean operators - AND, OR, NOT - can help you narrow down your search, and the library staff will be able to help you understand how to use these effectively. Sometimes you may be asked to pay for a journal article or book access. However, the library may be able to help you access it for free, so discuss the situation with them before you give up or pay unnecessarily. They may even be able to help you access a copy from another library via the Inter-Library Loans (ILL) scheme. If they can obtain the required resource from another library, it is usually free for the students. Never underestimate the knowledge of librarians. They are experts in finding evidence, and a workshop or discussion with them can significantly impact your development in this area.

Recommended reading

Staying Well and Safe at University by Dominique Thompson (2019) is part of the Student Well-being Series. It is intended to assist students in navigating the challenges that they may face while at university. The guide offers tips and resources to help you have a healthier and safer university experience.

Useful websites

RCNi well-being site includes resources offering support with managing stress and achieving work-life balance. It also site covers nursing students' experiences, financial and assignment management, self-care, and mental health.

https://rcni.com/nursing-standard/students/well-being

UCAS Mental Health and Well-being contains information and resources for students regarding mental health and well-being support at university.

https://www.ucas.com/undergraduate/student-life/mental-health-and-well-being

NURSING PLACEMENTS

Introduction

Your nursing placements are an essential link between theory learning and professional practice, allowing you to apply what you have learned in the classroom in various healthcare settings. This chapter will consider how to prepare for your early clinical experiences and flourish in every placement. We will discuss strategies and tips for maximising your placements, enhancing your learning, and developing meaningful professional relationships. Finding your voice and being accountable are integral to thriving in your placements. While expressing your thoughts and concerns may feel intimidating, as your confidence grows, you should more clearly recognise your contribution as part of the nursing team. This chapter will also consider difficulties that nursing students can sometimes encounter in placement, along with steps to resolve them.

Your first placement

Your first clinical placement is an exciting step towards becoming a nurse. It gives you a real-world understanding of your chosen profession and allows you to put the theoretical knowledge to use (Molesworth and Lewitt, 2016). It is an experience that many nurses will remember for the rest of their careers. However, it is natural to be full of nervous anticipation as your first placement approaches. The feeling will differ for each person, depending on whether you are familiar with healthcare settings and how you tend to cope with new situations. Nevertheless, almost everyone will feel some degree of trepidation as the first shift approaches. This section will consider some areas you can consider to help you prepare and have a positive experience during your first placement.

Do your research

When you receive your allocation, start learning everything you can about your placement. This approach will help you prepare and feel more informed when you begin the placement. Carry out some research into the healthcare setting and the type of care they provide. Your university should be able to provide background details about the area, and you will often be able to find further information online. Discussions with your nursing student peers who have previously been on placement in the same healthcare setting can be invaluable, and they can often provide advice and tips on what to expect. Your first placement could be in one of many different settings, including hospitals, nursing homes, clinics, and community health centres. Learn about the patients they serve, their services, and their values. Think about whether it is primarily a rural or urban service. What are the most prevalent health issues or challenges in that community? Understanding the larger social context can help inform your approach to patient care and highlight areas of health promotion to consider.

Once you have a good understanding of the placement setting, it can be helpful to take time to prepare for your placement experiences (Grace, 2016). Take time to think about the nursing skills you must display. Reflect on the fundamentals you have been learning about at university, and then consider how these might apply to the specific area you have been allocated. Are there any particular health issues or conditions that the patient population you will serve will require support with? Carry out some research into your specific needs and the nursing proficiencies you will need to display. Are there nursing procedures or proficiencies you are likely to be involved with? A nursing dictionary can help you understand words commonly used in the setting. This familiarisation can help improve understanding when discussing and handing over patient care. Becoming skilled in this new vocabulary will take time, but your efforts will help you feel more connected and less unsure. The more you invest in getting ready, the greater the sense of control and preparedness you will feel.

Activity 7.1: Nursing home placement

Nursing homes are often a placement area that student nurses will encounter at some point during their studies. Suppose you have not previously worked in a nursing home. In that case, it will likely be a new type of experience that varies from the acute and community settings that often come to mind when considering nursing roles. The learning environment within a nursing home will usually provide excellent opportunities to learn about person-centred care, enhance your communication skills with residents and their families, and navigate complex chronic disease management. This activity is intended to provide some ideas about how you can prepare for a nursing home placement. It will help you understand the healthcare setting, meaning you feel ready to meet your learning objectives once you commence a nursing home placement.

Begin by researching a nursing home within your local area. If the nursing home has a website, look it up to learn more about their philosophy of care and the services they offer. Consider finding reviews or news articles about the nursing home. This may provide information about events the nursing home has been involved with and other aspects of its place within the community. Next, consider chatting with peers who have previously had a nursing home placement. They may be able to provide information about what to expect and how to prepare for your first day. Study the health conditions that people in nursing homes may require support with. Dementia, arthritis, heart disease, and diabetes are all examples. Try taking a detailed look at dementia or another health condition to build on your existing knowledge. Understanding the pathophysiology, typical signs and symptoms and support required will help you meet the needs of residents in a nursing home environment. Remember that the goal of this activity is not to become an expert but to feel more prepared and confident about nursing home placements.

Questions

- *How did your perception of the nursing home environment change after conducting this research?*
- *Reflecting on the process, how effective would this approach be when preparing for a future placement?*

A suggested answer is given at the end of the chapter.

Once you have relevant background information, you may wish to find out the shift pattern you will be working on and details about the nursing staff that will supervise you. You can usually find placement contact details via university systems but check with your personal tutor if you are unsure. Most placements will be happy for you to contact them in advance of your first day but remember these are busy environments. If an immediate response is not received, it does not mean they are not looking forward to supporting you during the placement.

Practical preparation

Research the journey to your placement in advance so you know exactly how to be there on time. It can be an unpleasant experience rushing to a new placement while running late when you would prefer to be making a good first impression. If driving, check things like congestion at the times you will be travelling and parking arrangements. Remember that hospital car parks can get very busy, and there will be a charge for using them in some locations. Public transport times and routes will need to be scoped ahead of time, and sometimes a practice run can help put you at ease before the first day. If using another means of getting to placement, such as sharing a lift, ensure everything is agreed upon in pick-up times and places. You must prioritise your safety when travelling to and from placement and follow your university's guidance (RCN, 2023b). This is especially the case when travelling early in the morning or late at night when fewer people are around. It is worthwhile ensuring people you trust know your travel arrangements and that your phone is fully charged in case of delays or other problems. Stay alert to your surroundings, and remember that looking at your phone or listening to music through headphones can reduce your awareness. Always use reliable and trusted transportation. If driving, aim to park in a well-lit and busy area (Downey, 2023). Trust your instincts and take steps to exit the situation if something feels wrong or unsafe.

Remember to account for your physical and mental well-being when preparing for your first placement. It is essential to perform self-care to help you manage the stresses of being in an unfamiliar and busy environment. As discussed in Chapter 5, hydration and nutrition are vital for maintaining energy levels throughout the day, so bring a water bottle and some healthy snacks (Oliver, 2020). Also, before your first day, try to ensure you get a good night's sleep. Being well-rested will help you focus and perform better overall. If you are feeling overwhelmed, do not be afraid to seek support. Your practice supervisor, personal tutor, and peers are all excellent resources. From a practical point of view, it would be worth checking if you have any equipment or items that may be required during your first placement. Do you have a student identification badge you need to display? Are there pieces of helpful equipment that you may need, such as a washable fob watch? Finally, you must dress professionally, as will be discussed in more detail in the next section.

Recognise expectations

As a student nurse starting your first placement, you will be required to meet various expectations, not least of which is professionalism. You should seek to uphold the nursing profession's standards and values throughout your placement. You will likely learn about these in university, including dignity, trustworthiness, and compassion. You must follow the NMC (2018a) code of professional standards, ensuring respectful interactions with patients, their families, and healthcare colleagues. Use your communication skills with colleagues and patients, keeping in mind the various backgrounds and needs of those around you. You must respect patients' confidentiality and privacy, so never share personal or medical information without their permission. Always check with a registered nurse if you are unsure. Being proactive in your learning is also very important. While it may take time to become confident in asking for opportunities, try to accept every offer to learn something new. When you do not understand something, ask for clarification. Remember that every nurse started where you are now. Seek constructive feedback from your practice supervisors and peers, demonstrating active engagement in reflective practice to learn and grow throughout the placement.

Another expectation during your first placement is punctuality. Consistently being on time during your placement demonstrates dedication and dependability. If something unforeseen means you are running late, do not panic, as these things happen to everyone at times, but try to keep the placement updated where possible. Remember that delays and interruptions can have consequences for patient care. If you do not arrive for a shift without informing anyone, a senior member of the team will need to make enquiries to check you are safe and well, which can result in time away from their usual responsibilities. Check what the uniform requirements are for the placement you have been allocated. This can vary between community and in-patient settings. Deal with any issues relating to the uniform's size and fit well before placement. If you need to use a tailoring service, your university may be able to assist. Ensure your uniform is washed, ironed, neatly folded, and ready to wear.

Activity 7.2: Recognising expectations

This activity is designed to assist you in exploring the expectations that a clinical placement may have. The process will help prepare you for a successful placement experience. To start the activity, take 10 minutes to brainstorm the expectations the placement may have for you. Make a list of any expectations, inclusive of factors such as behaviours, attitudes, and skills. Do not think too long about each expectation; the aim here is to write down as many as come to mind. The emphasis here is not on being right or wrong but exploring the range of possible expectations. The next part of the activity is a reflection exercise. You should review the list and consider how prepared you are to meet each expectation. Try to be honest about areas where you are confident and need to improve. Now prepare a plan for each expectation where they have identified a potential gap in meeting placement expectations. The plan should outline the steps you will take to help develop in these areas. You may also consider how you expect the expectations to change as you progress through the placement. Remember that student nurses have many expectations placed upon them, and it will take time to recognise and meet all these. This activity should help you begin this process and improve your readiness for upcoming placement experiences.

Question

- *How important do you believe self-assessment and professional growth are in meeting expectations?*

A suggested answer is given at the end of the chapter.

The nursing uniform is central to professionalism (Daigle, 2018). There are often specific guidelines for wearing a uniform in public when travelling to and from placement. You must find out what the requirements are and adhere to them, coming across a senior nurse while wearing your uniform in an inappropriate setting is not ideal. Remember that you represent your university and profession, so aim to maintain the highest possible standards. There will likely be a uniform policy you can refer to concerning factors like how hair should be worn and the type of footwear that is permitted. Uniform guidelines are designed with infection control and prevention in mind (Owen et al., 2022). They must be followed, and try not to be influenced if you see others who choose not to follow uniform policy. They are responsible for any lack of professional practice they display. If you are on placement with another student, checking each other's uniforms can be worthwhile before starting the shift. It can be easy to forget something, so a quick check will help correct any issues before you begin performing patient care. Ask for clarification from your university if you are unsure about the uniform requirements for placement.

It is advisable that you do not use your phone on placement unless you are on a break. You may see other nurses doing it, but if you look at a nurse on their phone on the ward from a patient's point of view, it sends out the wrong message: that their social life is more important than their duty of care to patients. Leave your phone in a locker for patient confidentiality and infection control reasons.

Every hospital will have a policy on mobile phone use, but remember - you are there to learn not to keep up-to-date with your social media. While these expectations are necessary, remember that you are at an early stage of your learning journey. If you fall short, do not be too hard on yourself and take any feedback as an opportunity for development. Remind yourself that it is perfectly normal to be nervous or uncertain and that it is okay not to know everything during your first placement.

Flourishing in placement

Thriving in placement will require adaptability and resilience while integrating into the healthcare team. How you approach a placement will often influence your experiences. Seek to develop a learning mindset where each shift presents an opportunity to learn something new. Be inquisitive and aim to establish positive relationships with the people in the team. They are your supervisors and support system during your placement. Being respectful, helpful, and enthusiastic can go a long way towards creating a positive work environment. Feeling a sense of belonging is an integral part of a student nurse's experiences in placement (Levett-Jones and Lathlean, 2008). Belongingness is fostered when student nurses feel accepted by others within the placement area and have people to turn to if needed (Borrott et al., 2016). While you have a role to play when settling into the placement, remember that others have responsibilities for helping you integrate and meet your learning objectives. Many placements are welcoming and will facilitate positive experiences to help you establish a sense of belonging. We consider how to deal with situations where this is not the case later in the chapter.

At the end of the shift, take some time to think about what you have learned and experienced. This will help you consolidate your learning and process the experiences that you have been exposed to. Using a reflective diary can help structure your thoughts and help you use them to inform future practice. Reflective practice is integral to nursing because it will enable you to learn from experiences and improve your skills over time. Engaging with reflection will promote your self-awareness and professional development. Several reflective tools are recommended for student nurses. Gibbs' (1988) Reflective Cycle is one of the most popular reflective tools in nursing. It provides a clear structure for reflection with six stages: description, feelings, evaluation, analysis, conclusion, and action plan. This systematic approach can help you organise your thoughts and draw meaningful conclusions from your experiences. John's Model of Structured Reflection is another widely used reflective tool. This model is more in-depth and asks specific, guided questions at each stage of the reflection process. The framework is beneficial when reflecting on complex or emotionally charged situations, and it can help you delve deeper into your thoughts and feelings. If you are looking for a simple model, Borton's (1970) Development Framework is a straightforward yet effective model for healthcare professionals to use. It asks three questions: 'What?' 'So what?' 'Now what?' These questions encourage you to consider an experience, its implications and plan your next steps. It might be advantageous if you have limited time available.

Finding your voice

Finding your voice during placements is essential to your progression from student to professional. Your voice is important and can make a real difference in terms of patient care. Student nurses have a key role in patient advocacy which involves speaking up on behalf of others (Hall, Seldomridge and Allen, 2022). Because you will spend a lot of time with patients, they may feel comfortable expressing their needs with you. They may also feel more at ease speaking with you compared to a more senior nursing and medical team member. In consultation with your practice supervisor, you can use the information they share with you to enhance their care.

At times you may encounter care that falls below the expected standards. In these situations, it is essential to use your voice. Subtle responses may assist in improving care in some circumstances. These may include indirect challenges, showing concern for patients, and talking to approachable nurses or lecturers about the issues (Rees and Monrouxe, 2016). However, if you become concerned about poor care or identify problems that may jeopardise patient safety, you must report it as soon as possible. There will likely be a 'cause for concern' process that you can follow and seek support from experienced colleagues and university tutors as appropriate. You should be able to raise a concern without fear of reprisal, so ask for assistance if you believe you are being treated differently after raising a concern (Fagan, Lea and Parker, 2021). Remember that when you enter a placement area, you bring a fresh set of eyes, which can help you identify areas of good practice and those that require development.

Activity 7.3: Finding your voice

Moving from placement to placement can be challenging when integrating into the different teams you will encounter. Sometimes you may feel overlooked or unheard, especially when attempting to express your thoughts or concerns. However, it is essential to remember that you make a vital contribution to the team, bringing unique and valuable insights that can enhance patient care. This activity will lead you through a self-reflective process to improve your ability to share your perspectives with patients and colleagues. It helps you delve into a past experience, analyse your reactions, and imagine a different outcome to plan for similar situations that may arise. The goal is to empower you to confidently express your thoughts and ideas, enabling you to shape your learning experiences better. By the end of this activity, you should feel more able to articulate your points of view and promote open dialogue with colleagues.

Step 1: *The first step is to recall a recent situation from your placement or an alternative environment (e.g. in a previous job) in which you felt compelled to speak up but found it challenging. Remember as many details* *as possible, such as the context, the people involved, and the topic. You should carefully think about how you felt at the time.*

Step 2: *Now you have reflected on the situation, break down what kept you from speaking up. What about that situation made it difficult for you to express your thoughts? Was it the people involved, the circumstances, insecurities, or a combination of these factors? Make a list of your ideas.*

Step 3: *Recreate the situation but imagine yourself speaking up this time. What are your thoughts? How would you phrase it? Try making a script of the words you would have spoken.*

Step 4: *Try speaking the script out loud. Think about the tone of your voice, body language, and facial expressions as you talk. The aim is to stay calm, confident and in control as you speak. The goal here is not only to find your words but also to believe in them.*

Step 5: *The final step is to try speaking up the next time you feel strongly about something but are hesitant. This does not have to be in placement; it could be during a class in university. Try to do so in a similar manner to that described in Step 4. Consider whether it went as expected and how you feel after using your voice.*

Remember that communication is a skill that can be developed with practice. You can gain confidence in expressing your ideas and opinions over time.

Questions

- *What emotions did you feel when you remembered a situation where you could not voice your thoughts? How did these feelings influence your analysis and anticipated outcome?*

- *What strategies might you use in future to ensure that your voice is heard during placements?*

A suggested answer is given at the end of the chapter.

Confidence in your nursing practice will take time to develop. As you build your knowledge, skills, and experience, confidence levels should begin to rise. However, the development of confidence naturally fluctuates as you progress through your studies (Chesser-Smyth and Long, 2013). Your learning journey spans two interconnected landscapes: theory and practice. Combining these will lay the groundwork for improved confidence (Pront and McNeill, 2019). Avoid approaching them as two separate domains. While in placement, continue your engagement with theory, and this increased understanding will enable you to collaborate and converse with patients and colleagues more clearly. Aim to communicate clearly and professionally, sticking to the facts while maintaining a calm, composed demeanour. Often this will improve your ability to develop professional relationships and remain connected with various activities in the practice setting, such as handovers, multidisciplinary team conferences, and nursing procedures. While at university, reflect on your placement experiences during classes meaningfully. Your lecturers often design activities designed to facilitate this type of learning. Understanding nursing concepts and principles will solidify as you go deeper into topics. Improved comprehension across theory and practice will help you find your voice.

> ***Student insights***
>
> *"And the culture there was really like.. that you have to stand up for yourself. She also told me like, it can be quite hard, but like, that's just how it is."*
>
> *Student nurse research participant*
>
> *(Bril et al., 2022, p.387)*

Interactions with patients and their families are essential to developing your confidence (Molesworth, 2017). Patient responses and feedback on the standards of care they receive will provide insights into your progress as a nursing student. Even small indications of the difference you have made for a person can be a significant confidence booster. Even if the feedback indicates areas for improvement, it is an opportunity to learn and grow. This will make you more confident when interacting with patients and finding your voice as an essential contributor to their care (Ivany, 2012). Maintaining a positive outlook and believing in your abilities is crucial in developing confidence in nursing practice. There will inevitably be frustrations and demanding days but try to keep these in perspective; many student nurses will likely have encountered similar difficulties. Seeking guidance and support to persist through these challenges will be necessary. Another way you can use your voice is through placement evaluation. These can help inform aspects that are working well or need improvement to benefit future students. As you gain more experience and navigate the complexities of nursing care, your voice will gradually become more robust and impactful. It will be a journey of continuous self-improvement through which you will develop deep-seated confidence in your nursing practice.

Accountability

Whilst learning, everyone can make mistakes. A famous saying, often attributed to Niels Bohr (1885 – 1962), is that an expert may be described as a person who has made all the mistakes that can be made in their given field! If you make a mistake while on placement, own up to it as soon as possible. You will often find that whatever has happened can be rectified if reported immediately. Staying silent and hoping no one will notice can jeopardise patient care, and the guilt will make you feel much worse than owning up and facing the consequences. Every nurse has made mistakes, even the ones who deny this. In some respects, the latter are the ones to be wary of. They either have not noticed they have made mistakes to learn from or have side-stepped responsibility, which is not something to replicate. Most nurses can remember a drug error they have made. The guilt and fear of causing harm are gut-wrenching and can shake your confidence. However, speaking up straight away can avoid serious injury, while speaking to colleagues can support you and help prevent the same mistakes from being made by others. You may worry that your practice supervisor or peers will think less of you. In reality, experienced colleagues will generally appreciate your honesty and acknowledgement of a mistake. It will give them confidence that they can trust you, as you are truthful about your actions. Remember that you never tend to make the same mistake twice.

Dealing with problems

As we have previously considered in this chapter, almost every nursing student will encounter difficulties at some point during their placements. These challenges may include unwelcoming placement areas, demanding workloads, or failure to achieve learning outcomes. The earlier you detect and respond to a problem, the easier it will be to resolve. Do not ignore an issue causing you difficulty or discomfort in placement. Recognise it and begin to consider possible solutions.

You will encounter many different people during your placements. Sometimes communication difficulties and other interpersonal issues can arise. Minton and Birks (2019) and O'Flynn-Magee et al. (2020) show the unfortunate reality that nursing students can sometimes experience bullying within their placement settings. Such experiences can be very distressing and negatively impact confidence and performance. As Patel et al. (2022) noted, incivility from nursing staff within the placement area can also erode this sense of belonging. Additionally, an unsupportive learning environment can make you feel isolated, affecting your identity as a nurse (Molesworth, 2017). Various factors can contribute to these experiences, such as high patient-nurse ratios, staff shortages, or institutional culture. However, this does not mean it is acceptable for a student nurse to experience issues of this nature. Read the scenario for an example of such a situation. If you feel you are not being treated respectfully, a starting point is to have a conversation with the person involved. They may be unaware of the issue, and discussing it may result in a resolution. If the problem cannot be resolved or is more serious, it may be necessary to escalate it to someone more senior.

Scenario: Abdi

Abdi is a first-year student nurse who recently began his first placement at a medical ward. The nurses in the area seem nice enough, but he finds it hard to settle into the ward as the days pass. He is often referred to as 'the student', and they rarely use his name. When lunch break comes around, he is not invited to join the other staff in the social space and usually dines alone in the canteen. He starts to feel isolated, and although the nurses do not say anything rude towards him, he is beginning to feel invisible. Abdi is a confident person who used to run his own business and tries to engage with the staff. They engage with him at the time, but he does not seem able to form a professional connection that lasts beyond the moment. His self-confidence starts to ebb away, accompanied by increased stress due to the limited opportunities to share and discuss his placement experiences.

Abdi spends some time thinking about how to improve the situation. He decides not to give up or take the situation as a reflection of him as a person. Likely, the nurses are not intentionally making him feel this way. He begins by attempting to establish personal connections, striking up conversations during quiet moments and sharing a little about himself. He listened attentively and asked questions to learn more about his colleagues, expressing a genuine interest in getting to know them better. He also gently reinforces his identity by using his name more frequently in interactions, encouraging those around him to do the same. He politely told his practice supervisor he would like to join the other nurses at lunchtime. He explains that he contributes to patient care and would like to chat and socialise with the team. Abdi also has a backup plan if the situation worsens despite his efforts. This includes discussing the situation with his personal tutor and the charge nurse within the placement to see if they have any advice or can help ensure a more inclusive environment for students.

Abdi plans to provide feedback regarding his experiences within the placement evaluation which is completed after finishing. This will help to ensure that future students feel more a part of the team from the outset of the placement. The problematic experience fosters growth and resilience, providing Abdi with self-advocacy skills that will serve him throughout his nursing career.

Question

- *Reflecting on Abdi's scenario, how would you react if you were in a similar situation during your placement?*

A suggested answer is given at the end of the chapter.

If you encounter any form of bullying as a student, it is vital that it is not tolerated, and you should be supported to address it (Alshawush, Hallett and Bradbury-Jones, 2022). Sources of support may include speaking with your practice supervisor on placement, contacting your personal tutor, and utilising support services such as counselling or peer support groups. They can offer practical advice and emotional support. At times, the university and practice partners must take steps to ensure a safe and positive learning environment. They will jointly explore the best way to address the issues and ensure you are supported. It can be worth keeping a private note of the problems and the date and time of any incidents. These details may be required if the situation deteriorates or there is an investigation. It is also important to remember that the attitudes and behaviours of others do not reflect your worth or abilities as a nurse (Clarke et al., 2012). Try not to internalise negativity and do not let the difficulties cloud your view of other placements; remember that most offer excellent learning experiences.

Aside from interpersonal issues, the demanding nature of many placements can bring challenges. If you find that placement stresses are overwhelming, try identifying specific areas that are the main causes of how you feel. This can help set realistic goals and prioritise your tasks. Seek advice and guidance from those responsible for supervising your practice. It can also be helpful to speak with fellow student nurses about how you are feeling, sharing can help put things into perspective, and they may have hints and tips to assist.

Another difficulty that can arise is failure to meet your agreed objectives for the placement (Burden, Topping, and O'Halloran, 2018). It will naturally be discouraging if this occurs, but it is essential to remember that failure is a natural part of the learning process. Use this as an opportunity to consider your strengths and areas for improvement. Seek feedback from your supervisors to jointly create an action plan so you can work on the issues moving forward (Howard and Will, 2018). Dealing with problems can be stressful, so taking care of your mental and physical health is vital. For more information, see the self-care section in Chapter 5. Maintaining a positive attitude and resilience in the face of adversity is also essential. Remember that problems and challenges are all part of the learning process. They are chances for you to learn and grow. Every obstacle you overcome will help to make you a more capable and resilient nursing professional.

Conclusion

Each placement will be different and provide unique learning opportunities. From the excitement and apprehension of your first placement to your developing identity as a student nurse, it is through navigating these experiences that you will flourish in practice. As we have covered in this chapter, there are several things that you can do to prepare for success in your placements. The time you invest in undertaking research and practical preparations will pay off. It is essential to focus on accepting opportunities for learning and growth that they provide. As your confidence develops over time, you will find your voice and recognise your vital contribution to patient care and advocacy. You will also be well-prepared to meet expectations, be accountable and deal with problems that arise during your placements. This knowledge can influence your experiences in practice and may even lead to future job opportunities, which we explore in the next chapter.

Suggested answers

Activity 7.1

Undertaking this preparation may have enhanced your understanding of the complexities of nursing home environments. Your perceptions may have been shaped initially by limited personal experience. However, after conducting the research, you may have gained a better understanding of the role of nursing home care in supporting people with complex health conditions and social needs. You may also have discovered that nursing homes have a broader role to play in the community and residents' families. You would have become aware of nursing knowledge and values that will be required to provide person-centred care to meet the needs of residents. A deeper understanding of the nursing home environment should help you approach this placement with greater openness and preparedness.

Reflecting on the effectiveness of this research approach for future placements, you may recognise the usefulness of conducting preliminary research. It provides insights into the placement setting, relevant health conditions and the nursing care that will be carried out. Beyond this, it also encourages you to be a proactive learner and to lay the groundwork for making the most of the learning opportunities a placement may offer. This activity may help you recognise the significance of independent learning and may be a valuable approach for future placements.

Activity 7.2

While completing this activity, you may have discovered that self-assessment and continuous professional growth are essential in meeting your nursing placements' expectations. Recognising your strengths and areas for improvement may have highlighted the usefulness of taking time out for self-reflection. As you progress through your nursing studies, you may decide to repeat the activity to see how expectations and your ability to meet them change over time. This ongoing commitment to professional development ensures that you are constantly improving and adapting to meet the needs of patients and the changing healthcare landscape.

Activity 7.3

Remembering a time when you did not feel able to use your voice can bring forth a wide range of emotions. Frustration and disappointment may be present, along with feelings of inadequacy or self-doubt. These emotions are common in such situations, and most people will experience these feelings when reflecting upon them. Because of the negative emotions, you may become unduly negative about your actions and responses. However, it is essential to remember that building your confidence in speaking up can take time. Try to use emotions to help ensure a different outcome in future interactions. Channel your findings from this activity into positive forces that foster assertiveness and recognise the value you can bring by finding your voice.

You can employ various strategies to ensure your voice is heard during placements. First, preparing and practising key points before meetings or discussions may increase confidence in expressing your ideas. Second, actively seeking out opportunities to share your ideas and suggestions can make a difference, whether during a team meeting or a meeting with your practice supervisor. Third, work on understanding the importance of body language in communication. This includes maintaining eye contact, adopting an open posture, and confidently expressing oneself. This can help to ensure that your voice is heard. Finally, remember that student services (see Chapter 6) at the university can offer you guidance and support with communication and public speaking.

Scenario: Abdi

If you were in a situation similar to Abdi's during placement, you would likely have felt uneasy or disheartened at first. However, seeing Abdi's proactive approach may inspire you to try a similar technique. Conversations with the other nurses, expressing interest in their experiences, and sharing your background can all help establish a professional connection. If you notice that your name is not being used, you can gently remind people of it during interactions. To avoid being left out of social situations, ask if you could join your colleagues for lunch. Try not to internalise the problems as a reflection on you; there will be other factors at play, and the nurses may not even be aware of how you feel. If these steps do not result in an improved situation or if the situation worsens, you should consider seeking assistance. Discuss the issue with someone more senior so you can get guidance and support. While these actions may appear daunting, it is essential to remember that developing resilience is an aspect of professionalism (NMC, 2018d).

Recommended reading

Clinical Placements: A Pocket Guide by Kirstie Paterson and Jessica Wallar (2017) is a handy, pocket-sized book that provides valuable tips and advice to help students prepare for and maximise their practice learning experiences. It discusses placement preparation, learning opportunities, raising concerns, and reflection.

Reflective Practice for Nurses by Claire Boyd (2023) introduces many reflection models, core contexts, and principles. The book is designed for busy nursing professionals who want a quick overview of reflective practice and its benefits.

Useful websites

The ***RCN*** has a section on its website which focuses on bullying and harassment in the workplace and how to deal with it. Although mainly for registered nurses, it also has information for student nurses. There are links to other resources and sources of support.
https://www.rcn.org.uk/Get-Help/RCN-advice/bullying-and-harassment

The ***RCN*** provides an audio series for nursing students by Dr Sharon Black, a nurse educator and the RCN's professional lead for

education and leadership. The series discusses how to prepare for placements, how to deal with nerves, and how to maximise learning opportunities.
https://www.rcn.org.uk/magazines/Advice/2023/Jan/Placements-A-Students-Survival-Guide

The ***RCN*** also provides guidance on prioritising personal safety in the workplace. It emphasises employers' legal duty to protect employees' health and safety and highlights the importance of risk assessments and implementing measures to reduce risks.
https://www.rcn.org.uk/Get-Help/RCN-advice/prioritising-personal-safety

CAREER OPTIONS

Introduction

One significant advantage of becoming a nurse is that it will provide numerous career opportunities across various specialities and settings. The contribution of nursing extends across many areas of society. It includes essential nursing roles in public healthcare alongside roles in many less prominent sectors. This chapter introduces you to the diversity of nursing opportunities to help inform your understanding of the different career options. While it may be tempting to decide early about the type of nursing you want to work in, experimenting with other areas before making a decision can be beneficial. We will explore the benefits of taking your time and finding the right fit for your preferences and circumstances. When considering your choices, it is critical to consider factors such as finding the right team and accounting for the pay and conditions offered by different roles. This chapter intends to help you navigate your unique path in the nursing profession by providing insightful information about career options ahead of you.

A wealth of opportunities

As you begin your nursing career, it is worth recognising the wealth of opportunities it offers. Nursing is a diverse profession encompassing a wide range of specialities, roles, and environments. As you will find throughout your studies, nurses work in acute settings, community settings, schools, health centres, prisons, and nursing homes. There are also roles you may not have considered, such as education, policy, research, management, and government positions. We'll now explore some of these areas.

Many nurses work outside of NHS settings in sectors such as business, global health organisations and the military. In the business world, particularly within pharmaceutical and medical equipment companies, you can find nurses working in various roles. They may serve as clinical consultants, using their expertise to inform the development, testing, and marketing of new drugs or medical devices. Major pharmaceutical and medical companies such as GlaxoSmithKline, Philips, B. Braun, and AstraZeneca employ nurses to contribute to their research, marketing, and sales efforts. These roles allow nurses to use their clinical knowledge in a business context which can provide different rewards and challenges to working in the public sector. Nurses should be aware that working with the commercial sector can bring conflicts of interest, so always check workplace and professional guidance (RCN, 2023c). Nurses also make contributions to the entertainment industry, particularly in the realm of film and television production. Their real-life experience and expertise can be invaluable for accurate and realistic portrayal of healthcare scenarios. This helps to enhance the authenticity of the content and can also but can also play a role in educating the public about health issues and the nursing profession.

Benefits and insurance services are another sector where nurses use their knowledge to assess claims and support decisions regarding coverage and the unique requirements of different people. As part of aeromedical evacuation teams, nurses provide critical care during transport for patients who must be moved across national or international boundaries. Another important avenue for the profession is nursing in the military. Nurses can join the Royal Navy, Army, or Royal Air Force. They provide physical and mental health care to active-duty military veterans and their dependents (Conley, 2014). They also provide healthcare to the public in the NHS, which helps them develop and maintain their skills. Nurses in the military perform many of the same tasks as civilian nurses, such as patient care, health promotion, and disease prevention. The nature of the military will also require them to operate in more difficult and unpredictable conditions, especially during conflict.

Nurses often play a central role in research teams. Your university lecturers will often be involved in research as part of their role.

Organisations such as the National Institute for Health Research (2023) frequently fund nurses to conduct studies that advance nursing practice and improve patient care. Many nurses advance into leadership positions overseeing patient care, managing nursing staff, and coordinating services within their units or departments. They may also be involved in strategic planning, quality assurance, and risk management. Nurses also shape healthcare delivery and policies at the organisational and national levels. Some nurses may advance to executive positions, such as a Nurse Executive or Director of Nursing in an NHS trust or board, where they can influence organisational strategies and operations. At the national level, there is the role of Chief Nursing Officer (Cummings et al., 2017) for Scotland, England, Wales, and Northern Ireland, who advises on nursing issues for each nation. Nurses in these roles actively shape and influence healthcare legislation, policy, and standards. Many other nurses work alongside them to govern and lead through support and advisory roles.

Activity 8.1: Exploring your career options

This activity aims to assist you with exploring the different career options available once you complete your studies. It will help you make informed decisions about your future nursing career. Start the activity by reflecting upon your professional interests and passions. Try thinking about the parts of the nursing programme that you have found most engaging. Take note of the nursing topics and placement areas that stand out. Keep it broad at this stage and do not exclude areas such as research, education, or leadership. Once you have a note of these areas, try to imagine where you would like your nursing career to be in five years. Write down any long-term goals that come to mind when considering your future. Next, you should identify one or two nursing career paths matching your interests and long-term goals. Explore what is involved in the selected areas by undertaking some online research. You may also wish to discuss your plans with your personal tutor, practice supervisors or peers to learn from their experiences, particularly if they know the relevant area of practice. Focus on identifying the role responsibilities, any required additional qualifications or training that may be needed, working conditions, potential employers, and career progression opportunities. Finally, imagine yourself five years in the future to visualise the daily responsibilities, challenges, and accomplishments that may come with following your interests and long-term goals. This process should assist you in evaluating your career path decisions and help you make informed decisions about your future.

Question

- *Did you encounter any career paths you were unaware of or had not considered?*

A suggested answer is given at the end of the chapter.

Each area of nursing offers a unique opportunity to broaden your skills and knowledge while making a difference in various aspects of people's lives. Remember that new opportunities will continue to emerge in the fast-changing healthcare landscape. Technological advancements are paving the way for roles in telehealth and informatics, and the increased emphasis on preventative care and population health has resulted in more opportunities in public health nursing. The Covid 19 pandemic placed further focus on this crucial field. Nursing offers many opportunities, whether you are interested in direct patient care, research, education, or leadership. With so many options, you should be able to find a path that suits your interests and strengths.

Do not commit early

You may feel pressure to choose a specific career path in the early stages of your nursing career. Many nursing students have a particular area of nursing they want to pursue even before they start their education. While having direction may be beneficial, keep an open mind and avoid committing too soon. One of the best advantages of nursing is its adaptability and the wide range of opportunities it offers. Keeping your options open will assist with gaining a broader understanding of the field, identifying your strengths, discovering your interests, and determining where your passion lies. Each new placement will provide different experiences and give you new insights into the profession. You will learn more about various patient populations, healthcare settings, and specialities, which will help you make career decisions. As they progress through their studies, many student nurses find themselves changing the area where they want to work upon registration (Stevens, 2011). Nursing is a dynamic profession constantly evolving and progressing. Societal and technological changes occur, as do healthcare systems and nursing roles. Remember that your early years in nursing are about personal and professional development. There is no rush to commit to a specific job until you are approaching registration.

Student insights

"I didn't think I would enjoy my community placement as I am used to working in the hospital. It was really interesting going into different people's homes and caring for them at home. The nurse had a great way with the patients and I learnt a lot. I'm actually thinking I should work in community when I finish [nursing studies]!"

Luciana, Student Nurse (Adult Field)

Joining the right team

Joining the right team will be important in finding success and fulfilment in your nursing career. The type of team you join will likely significantly impact your job satisfaction, professional growth, and work-life balance. While on each placement, consider whether you would like to work in that area. Speak to the team about their experiences. The more you can learn about different options, the more informed you will be when it comes to finding a job at the end of your nurse education. Look for a team that shares your values and beliefs; do they approach patient care, professional development and teamwork in a way that fits your perspective and priorities? Aligning with a team's values will help you feel more connected and committed. An ideal team creates a supportive atmosphere that respects all its members' views and contributions (Dickerson and Latina, 2017). A positive environment will facilitate collaboration and support you during setbacks while celebrating your successes.

Activity 8.2: Learn about the team

This activity is designed to help you evaluate potential teams you may join after registration as a nurse. It focuses on essential factors such as support, culture, and leadership. You should begin by listing their expectations and preferences for a team. What sort of environment do you like to work in? When completing this part of the activity, consider the types of teams you want to work in. For example, do you prefer large social teams, small close-knit teams, or individual working? Think about the level of support you would like, the type of culture they thrive in, and their preferred leadership style. Now identify different teams and environments you may work in once qualified. You might want to revisit your notes from Activity 8.1 when deciding. Reflect on your placement experiences, if appropriate, and carry out some research by speaking with current or former members of these teams about their experiences. You should concentrate on gathering information on the factors of the team's support, culture, and leadership. Completing this activity should provide a more nuanced understanding of what to look for in a group and help you choose a team that suits your attributes and preferences.

Questions

- *Did you discover any practices or characteristics you had not previously considered but now see as crucial in a team during your research?*
- *Based on your research and reflection, which aspects of team selection are you willing to compromise, and which are non-negotiable for you?*

A suggested answer is given at the end of the chapter.

Effective leadership in healthcare plays an essential role in shaping positive outcomes for patients and team members (Cummings et al., 2021). Leaders set the tone for the team and wider culture can significantly impact your experiences. Is the leader fair, open, and supportive? Consider how the nurses and other members of the group are treated. Look at whether the leader encourages and supports professional development. Is there evidence of in-service training, support programmes, opportunities to attend conferences or workshops, or assistance for formal education?

Diverse teams improve representation and bring differing perspectives, improving patient care, and enhancing team working (Lerman et al., 2022). Ethnicity, age, culture, and educational background can all contribute to diversity. A positive and diverse work environment with effective leadership will often indicate high job satisfaction and staff retention. Review the different types of teams you encounter during your education and use this information to help shape your decisions when selecting a team to work in once you are qualified. Being on the right team entails an environment where you can thrive, grow, and find fulfilment.

Pay and conditions

Pay and working conditions are critical factors when weighing your nursing career options. These elements can significantly impact your job satisfaction, work-life balance, and overall well-being. As discussed in Chapter 1, nurses' pay in the UK can vary depending on role, location, speciality, experience, and employer type. The private sector opportunities discussed in the first section of this chapter can bring higher, but it is vital to consider the overall benefits package, job security, and opportunities for professional development. There are also opportunities for increased pay for working unsocial hours or in high-cost areas such as London (BMJ Health Careers, 2022). The physical and psychological aspects of your workplace are essential to consider. When exploring your career options, look into workplace safety, access to necessary equipment and resources, and job demands such as shift patterns and working hours. Think about how these may affect your current circumstances as well as any future personal, professional, or family plans that you have.

Scenario: Gabriela

Gabriela is a 51-year-old newly qualified mental health nurse at the start of her career as a registered nurse. She has chosen to specialise in acute mental health care to support people in their most vulnerable moments. Gabriela knows the challenges and rewards of working in this demanding setting and thought long and hard about whether she should work in the acute mental health service as a permanent full-time employee or as a bank/agency nurse. Both have distinct advantages and disadvantages. Gabriela weighed up her career objectives, financial considerations, and personal circumstances. As a full-time employee, she would have greater job security and stability. A regular, fixed income would allow her to plan her finances better when compared with not being on the payroll. Full-time employees can access benefits like sick, maternity, and holiday pay. Furthermore, Gabriela's employer would significantly contribute to her pension, helping ensure her future financial security. She would also have more opportunities for professional development and advancement as a permanent staff member.

On the other hand, working full-time as a permanent staff member may limit her flexibility in finding a balance between her professional and personal lives. As a bank or agency nurse, she would have far greater flexibility with where and when she works, choosing her shifts as desired. This may allow her to achieve a better work-life balance and provide her with diverse experiences as she works in different settings. Agency nursing can be more financially profitable regarding the amount earned each month due to higher hourly rates, especially when working unsocial hours or on short notice. However, Gabriela knows these advantages need to be evaluated against fewer workplace protections, inconsistency in work, and less generous pension arrangements. She could see the value of each approach but ultimately decided that the job security, consistent income, and pension benefits that come with permanent employment were most important.

Question

- *How important is work-life balance to you, and how does this weigh against the benefits of job security and a regular income?*

A suggested answer is given at the end of the chapter.

Workload and stress levels are important considerations with healthcare workers experiencing increasing challenges in these areas over recent years (House of Commons, 2021). Check what employers are putting in place to reduce stress and improve nurses' working conditions. As you will know through placements, nurses frequently work long shifts, nights, weekends, and holidays, which can interfere with work-life balance. If this is an issue for you, look for roles and settings that provide more flexible or predictable work schedules. When thinking about your future career, it is essential to consider the pay and overall package. This should include opportunities for advancement, the nature of the work, and how it fits with your personal circumstances and lifestyle. Job satisfaction and well-being are often as important as the salary.

Conclusion

Each career opportunity that nursing provides is unique and valuable in its own way. It is a profession that allows you to choose from many different career options, more than many other vocations offer. We hope this chapter has outlined various opportunities available to you in your career journey, especially those you may not have already considered. This awareness of different roles should help ensure you can always find a path that aligns with your interests, values, and personal circumstances. Remember that there are advantages to taking your time and not committing right away. Each placement will give you an improved understanding of the nature of nursing work that suits you best. This includes important factors such as jointing the right time and considering the pay and working conditions. Having said all of that, it is worth remembering that nursing is a commitment to caring for others and not just a job. It will offer unique opportunities to make a genuine difference in people's lives. Choose a career path that will provide personal and professional fulfilment.

Suggested answers

Activity 8.1

While completing this activity, you may have discovered several career paths that you were previously unaware of or had not considered. Nursing offers so many specialisations and career opportunities that the different options are worth considering. These may not be commonly considered during your studies but may provide unique and rewarding career opportunities. Learning about unfamiliar nursing roles may have broadened your understanding of the profession, demonstrating its versatility and scope. It may have shown that nursing is not limited to the bedside but extends into various sectors such as legal, research, education, policy-making, and many others. The diversity of roles means you can significantly impact as a nurse in different professional spheres.

Activity 8.2

After completing this activity, you may think more deeply about team characteristics that are important to you. It may have assisted you in thinking about matching your team preferences to the career options that will lie ahead of you upon qualification. It may have provided further insights into factors such as leadership and culture regarding the teams that choose to join. As you may have come to appreciate during your placements, joining the right group is essential when considering your next career step. Taking time to match your preferences and values to the available teams will likely pay off in terms of finding the best fit for you.

When it comes to aspects you would be willing to compromise on when selecting a team, it could be a combination of personal preferences and professional development. For example, you may be ready to join a larger team you would prefer if you knew it will be a supportive environment promoting learning and professional growth. You may prioritise a collaborative culture that fosters inclusivity and respect over all other factors. Whatever your thoughts, it is crucial to recognise that the team you join has the potential to significantly impact areas such as job satisfaction, stress levels, and overall career trajectory.

Scenario: Gabriela

Your decision would depend on your personal situation, career goals, and life priorities. You may answer that work-life balance is essential. You know nursing can be emotionally and physically demanding and can lead to exhaustion. You know that work-life balance will help you recharge, avoid fatigue, and improve care standards. In a high-stress profession like nursing, ensuring you have interests and time for personal relationships can be critical to your well-being. Bank nursing and agency nursing can offer greater flexibility and choice over your working patterns. Equally, having job security and a stable income that comes with permanent employment can be valuable. These factors allow you to plan your life and meet your financial obligations, providing peace of mind which is also vital for your well-being. Remember that some employers will have flexible and family-friendly workplace policies in place. It is a balancing act, so consider how different employment options align with your personal and professional needs.

Recommended reading

Leadership and Management in Healthcare by Neil Gopee and Jo Galloway (2017) discuss routes towards effective leadership and management. It includes action points, case studies, and guidelines that help apply leadership and management theory to different care settings.

Useful websites

NHS Health Careers provides information on various healthcare careers for different types of nursing. It details the roles, entry requirements, skills needed, and career development opportunities in nursing. There are also stories from people in different nursing roles. ***https://www.healthcareers.nhs.uk/explore-roles/nursing/***

The ***RCN*** has a careers resource that provides information on professional development and work opportunities for nurses. Realistic scenarios demonstrate how to switch careers, the education and training needed, and the prospects. Case studies and videos or podcasts of people in that role accompany each scenario. ***https://www.rcn.org.uk/professional-development/nursing-careers-resource***

CONCLUSION

As we near the end of *The Ultimate Guide to Becoming a Nurse*, it should be clear that you are on an exciting and rewarding journey. We started with invaluable information that is useful to know before beginning nurse education. Various routes in the profession were considered, along with different fields of nursing and associated pay scales and qualifications. Next, we explore how to choose a university that fits your personal and professional goals and the practical steps you should take before beginning a nursing programme. This included essential areas such as funding, gathering the necessary information and undertaking appropriate reading. Transitioning to university life is an exciting change that may come with a degree of apprehension. This book provides information to help you navigate this new environment, explaining in straightforward and open terms how university works, the clinical skills you will learn during the early stages and the central concept of patient-centred care. The chapter titled 'achieving success' discussed NMC requirements and tips for passing assessment and managing your workload. Nurse education can be demanding and stressful. We have presented various strategies to support your well-being, from developing effective study habits to self-care for maintaining your mental and physical health.

Your placements have the potential to be transformative experiences. These real-world encounters enable you to apply theory to practice, develop your skills and develop the professional values that come with being a nurse. The 'nursing placements' chapter outlines how to make the most of your first placement with practical tips and information. Details about how to find your voice as a valued member of the term were explained, showing this will emerge as you become more confident in your knowledge and skills. Student nurses can encounter problems in placement areas, and this was discussed with reference to relevant evidence. A key message from this section is that you are not alone and to speak up early if you encounter poor care or attitudes. The final chapter explored the plethora of nursing careers and opportunities, including less typical nursing roles. As you finish this book, remember that nursing is a profession. It comes with a lifelong commitment to making a real difference in people's lives. We hope this book has provided valuable insights into how to become a nurse and change your passion into a professional career. It will be a life-changing journey, and we wish you every success with your dream of becoming a nurse!

REFERENCES

Abu Shahim, M. R., Shaudi, L. S., Zainudin, Z. N. and Kamarul, M. S. (2021) Online counselling services: University students' perception. Turkish Journal of Computer and Mathematics Education, Vol: 12(4), pp. 1173–1181. https://doi.org/10.17762/turcomat.v12i4.630

Alharbi, Kuhn, L. and Morphet, J. (2020) Undergraduate nursing students' adoption of the professional identity of nursing through social media use: A qualitative descriptive study. Nurse Education Today, Vol: 92, pp. 1-8. https://doi.org/10.1016/j.nedt.2020.104488

Alshawush, Hallett, N. and Bradbury-Jones, C. (2022) The impact of transition programmes on workplace bullying, violence, stress and resilience for students and new graduate nurses: A scoping review. Journal of Clinical Nursing, Vol: 31(17-18), pp. 2398–2417. https://doi.org/10.1111/jocn.16124

Andrewartha, L. and Harvey, A. (2017) Employability and student equity in higher education: The role of university careers services.

Australian Journal of Career Development, Vol: 26(2), pp. 71–80. https://doi.org/10.1177/1038416217718365

Attia, N. M. and Abdelwahid, A. E. A. (2020) Grit, Self-Regulation and Self-Efficacy as Predictors of Academic Procrastination among Nursing Students. International Journal of Nursing Education, Vol: 12(1), pp. 130-135. https://doi.org/10.37506/ijone.v12i1.3720

Badri Gargari, R., Sabouri, H. and Norzad, F. (2011) Academic procrastination: the relationship between causal attribution styles and behavioral postponement. Iranian journal of psychiatry and behavioral sciences, Vol: 5(2), pp. 76–72.

Blackburn, R., Johnson, K. G. and Chaveleh, S. (2020) Clinical Journal of Oncology Nursing, Vol: 24 (1), pp. 103-106. doi: 10.1188/20.CJON.103-106

BMJ Health Careers (2022) Guide to London NHS pay (Agenda for Change) 2021/2022. [Online] Available: https://healthjobs.bmj.com/article/guide-to-london-nhs-pay-agenda-for-change-2021-2022/ [Accessed: 03 February 2023].

Borrott, N., Day, G. E., Sedgwick, M. and Levett-Jones, T. (2016) Nursing students' belongingness and workplace satisfaction: Quantitative findings of a mixed methods study. Nurse Education Today, Vol: 45, pp. 29–34. https://doi.org/10.1016/j.nedt.2016.06.005

Boyd, C. (2023) Reflective Practice for Nurses. Chichester: Wiley Blackwell

Braine, M. E. and Parnell, J. (2011) Exploring student's perceptions and experience of personal tutors. Nurse Education Today, Vol: 31(8), pp. 904–910. https://doi.org/10.1016/j.nedt.2011.01.005

Bril, I., Boer, H. J., Degens, N. and Fleer, J. (2022) Nursing students' experiences with clinical placement as a learning environment for assertiveness: a qualitative interview study. Teaching and Learning in Nursing, Vol: 17(4), pp. 383–391. https://doi.org/10.1016/j.teln.2022.04.006

Bryant, J., Matthews, G. and Walton, G. (2009) Academic libraries and social and learning space: A case study of Loughborough University Library, UK. Journal of Librarianship and Information Science, Vol: 41(1), pp. 7–18. https://doi.org/10.1177/0961000608099895

Burden, S. Topping, A. E. and O'Halloran, C. (2018) Mentor judgements and decision-making in the assessment of student nurse competence in practice: A mixed-methods study. Journal of Advanced Nursing, Vol: 74(5), pp. 1078–1089. https://doi.org/10.1111/jan.13508

Chamberlain, D. (2023) How to Complete Your UCAS Application – 2024 Entry. Bath: Trotman Education.

Chesser-Smyth, P. and Long, T. (2013) Understanding the influences on self-confidence among first-year undergraduate nursing students in Ireland. Journal of Advanced Nursing, Vol: 69(1), pp. 145–157. https://doi.org/10.1111/j.1365-2648.2012.06001.x

Christiansen, A., Salamonson, Y., Crawford, R., McGrath, B., Roach, D., Wall, P., Kelly, M. and Ramjan, L. M. (2019) "Juggling many balls": Working and studying among first-year nursing students. Journal of Clinical Nursing, Vol: 28(21-22), pp. 4035–4043. https://doi.org/10.1111/jocn.14999

Clarke, C. (2014) Promoting the 6Cs of nursing in patient assessment. Nursing Standard, Vol: 28(44), pp. 52–59.

https://doi.org/10.7748/ns.28.44.52.e7967

Clarke, C. Kane, D. J., Rajacich, D. L. and Lafreniere, K. D. (2012) Bullying in Undergraduate Clinical Nursing Education. The Journal of Nursing Education, Vol: 51(5), pp. 269–276. https://doi.org/10.3928/01484834-20120409-01

Conley, C. (2014) Military nurses' growing role. Nursing Standard, Vol: 29(8), p. 13. https://doi.org/10.7748/ns.29.8.13.s17

Cottrell, S. (2018) Mindfulness for Students. London: Palgrave.

Cottrell, S. (2019) The Study Skills Handbook (5th ed.). London: Palgrave.

Cummings, G. G., Lee, S., Tate, K., Penconek, T., Micaroni, S. P. M., Paananen, T. and Chatterjee, G. E. (2021) The essentials of nursing leadership: A systematic review of factors and educational interventions influencing nursing leadership. International Journal of Nursing Studies, Vol: 115, pp. 1-14. https://doi.org/10.1016/j.ijnurstu.2020.103842

Cummings, J., McArdle, C., McQueen, F. and White, J. (2017) UK Chief Nursing Officers: shaping the future of the profession. British Journal of Nursing, Vol: 26(9), pp. 498–500. https://doi.org/10.12968/bjon.2017.26.9.498

Daigle, A. (2018) Professional image and the nursing uniform. The Journal of Continuing Education in Nursing, Vol: 49(12), pp. 555–557. https://doi.org/10.3928/00220124-20181116-06

Delves-Yates, C. (2022) Essentials of Nursing Practice. London: Sage.

Dickerson, J. and Latina, A. (2017) Team nursing: A collaborative approach improves patient care. Nursing, Vol: 47(10), pp. 16–17. https://doi.org/10.1097/01.NURSE.0000524769.41591.fc

Downey, A. (2023) Many nurses still face unsafe parking and journeys to work. [Online] Available: https://rcni.com/nursing-standard/newsroom/news/many-nurses-still-face-unsafe-parking-and-journeys-to-work-195266 https://commonslibrary.parliament.uk/research-briefings/cbp-8593/[Accessed: 08 August 2023].

Drewery, D. W., Westlund Stewart, N. and Wilson, A. W. (2022) Engagement in Mindfulness Exercises during Large Lectures and Students' Writing Self-Efficacy. The Canadian Journal for the Scholarship of Teaching and Learning, Vol: 13(1), pp. 1–12. https://doi.org/10.5206/cjsotlrcacea.2022.1.10945

Duffett-Leger, L., Beck, A. J., Siddons, A., Bright, K. S. and Alix Hayden, K. (2022) What Do We Know About Interventions to Prevent Low Back Injury and Pain Among Nurses and Nursing Students? A Scoping Review. Canadian Journal of Nursing Research, Vol: 54(4), pp. 392–439. https://doi.org/10.1177/08445621211047055

EBSCO (2023) CINAHL. [Online] Available: https://www.ebsco.com/products/research-databases/cinahl-database https://commonslibrary.parliament.uk/research-briefings/cbp-8593/ [Accessed: 08 August 2023].

El-Sharkawy, A. M., Bragg, D., Watson, P., Neal, K., Sahota, O., Maughan, R. J. and Lobo, D. N. (2016) Hydration amongst nurses and doctors on-call (the HANDS on prospective cohort study) Clinical Nutrition. Vol: 35(4), pp. 935–942. https://doi.org/10.1016/j.clnu.2015.07.007

Emery, C. (2014) Embrace essay writing as a holistic process. Nursing Standard, Vol: 29(4), p. 74.

Equality Act (2010) [Online] Available:

Http://www.legislation.gov.uk/ukpga/2010/15/contents [Accessed: 21 April 2020]

Fagan, A., Lea, J. and Parker, V. (2021) Student nurses' strategies when speaking up for patient safety: A qualitative study. Nursing & Health Sciences, Vol: 23(2), pp. 447–455. https://doi.org/10.1111/nhs.12831

Fawkes, and Moore, J. (2019) Newly registered nurses' experiences of delivering patient education in an acute care setting: an exploratory study. Journal of Research in Nursing, Vol: 24(8), pp. 556–567. https://doi.org/10.1177/1744987119869770

Gamble, S. C., Worth, T., Gilroy, P. and Newbold, S. (2020) Students as Co-authors of an Academic Development Service: A Case Study of the Study Skills Service at the University of Bristol. The New Review of Academic Librarianship, Vol: 26(2-4), pp. 275–290. https://doi.org/10.1080/13614533.2020.1784760

Garrett, B., Ong, P. and Galdas, P. (2022) Clinical Pocket Reference for Nurses (4th ed.). Oxford: Clinical Pocket Reference.

Gopee, N. and Galloway, J. (2017) Leadership and Management in Healthcare. (3rd ed.). London: Sage.

Grace, S., McLeod, G., Streckfuss, J., Ingram, L. and Morgan, A. (2016) Preparing health students for interprofessional placements. Nurse Education in Practice, Vol: 17, pp. 15–21. https://doi.org/10.1016/j.nepr.2016.02.001

Green, M. P. (2020) Inclusive Library Service to Individuals with Mental Illnesses and Disorders. The International Journal of Information, Diversity, & Inclusion, Vol: 4(1), pp. 119–126. https://doi.org/10.33137/ijidi.v4i1.32500

Guardian (2023) University Guide: The best UK universities 2023

– rankings. [Online] Available: https://www.theguardian.com/education/ng-interactive/2022/sep/24/the-guardian-university-guide-2023-the-rankings [Accessed: 03 July 2023].

Guendelman, S., Medeiros, S. and Rampes, H. (2017) Mindfulness and Emotion Regulation: Insights from Neurobiological, Psychological, and Clinical Studies. Frontiers in psychology, Vol: 8(220), pp. 1 - 23. https://doi.org/10.3389/fpsyg.2017.00220

Hall, N., Seldomridge, L. and Allen, K. (2022) Using Toolkits to Improve Students' Skills in Advocacy. The Journal of Nursing Education, Vol: 61(10), pp. 599–602. https://doi.org/10.3928/01484834-20220417-05

Hall, S. S. and Zygmunt, E. (2021) Dislocated College Students and the Pandemic: Back Home Under Extraordinary Circumstances. Family relations, Vol: 70(3), pp. 689–704. https://doi.org/10.1111/fare.12544

Haugh, K. H. (2015) Head-to-toe: Organizing your baseline patient physical assessment. Nursing, Vol: 45(12), pp. 58–61. https://doi.org/10.1097/01.NURSE.0000473396.43930.9d

Health Education and Improvement Wales (2022) [Online] Guidance for Pre-registration Nursing Degree Programmes. Available: https://heiw.nhs.wales/files/pre-registration-nursing-degree-funding-route-guidance-20221/ [Accessed: 14 February 2023]

Heinrich, D. and O'Connell, K. (2023) The Effects of Mindfulness Meditation on Nursing Students' Stress and Anxiety Levels. Nursing Education Perspectives, Publish Ahead of Print. doi: 10.1097/01.NEP.0000000000001159

Holt, P. J. and Dixon, J. (2022) NMC standards: a holistic approach to nursing care. [Online] Available: https://www.nursingtimes.net/opinion/nmc-standards-a-holistic-approach-to-nursing-care-09-12-2022/ [Accessed: 11 May 2023].

House of Commons (2021) Workforce burnout and resilience in the NHS and social care. [Online] Available: https://committees.parliament.uk/publications/6158/documents/68766/default/ [Accessed: 03 February 2023].

Howard, L. and Will, B. (2018) A collaborative strategy for clinical performance feedback. Teaching and Learning in Nursing, Vol: 13(3), pp. 141–144. https://doi.org/10.1016/j.teln.2018.02.001

Irish, L. A., Kline, C. E., Gunn, H. E., Buysse, D. J. and Hall, M. H. (2015) The role of sleep hygiene in promoting public health: A review of empirical evidence. Sleep medicine reviews, Vol: 22, pp. 23–36. https://doi.org/10.1016/j.smrv.2014.10.001

Ivany, E. (2012) Finding your voice as a student nurse. British Journal of Nursing, Vol: 21(13), pp. 826–826. https://doi.org/10.12968/bjon.2012.21.13.826

Keogh, K. (2014) Shift work and vending machines to blame for poor workplace diet: Nurses are struggling with their weight as the pressures of the job leave little time for healthy eating, a Nursing Standard survey reveals. Nursing Standard, Vol: 29(8), pp. 14–15. https://doi.org/10.7748/ns.29.8.14.s19

Kim, S., Mayer, C. and Jones, C. B. (2021) Relationships between nurses' experiences of workplace violence, emotional exhaustion and patient safety. Journal of Research in Nursing, Vol: 26(1-2), pp. 35–46. https://doi.org/10.1177/1744987120960200

Kononova, A. G. and Yuan, S. (2017) Take a Break: Examining

College Students' Media Multitasking Activities and Motivations During Study- or Work-Related Tasks. Journalism and Mass Communication Educator, Vol: 72(2), pp. 183–197. https://doi.org/10.1177/1077695816649474

Kotera, Y., Cockerill, V., Chircop, J. G. E. and Forman, D. (2021) Mental health shame, self-compassion and sleep in UK nursing students: Complete mediation of self-compassion in sleep and mental health. Nursing Open, Vol: 8(3), pp. 1325–1335. https://doi.org/10.1002/nop2.749

Kumar, and Jin, Y. (2022) Impact of nurses' emotional labour on job stress and emotional exhaustion amid COVID-19: The role of instrumental support and coaching leadership as moderators. Journal of Nursing Management, Vol: 30(7), pp. 2620–2632. https://doi.org/10.1111/jonm.13818

Lepp, A., Barkley, J. E., Karpinski, A. C. and Singh, S. (2019) College Students' Multitasking Behavior in Online Versus Face-to-Face Courses. SAGE Open, Vol: 9(1), 215824401882450–. https://doi.org/10.1177/2158244018824505

Lerman, C., Hughes-Halbert, C., Falcone, M., Gosky, D. M., Jensen, R. A., Lee, K. P., Mitchell, E., Odunsi, K., Pegher, J. W., Rodriguez, E., Sanchez, Y., Shaw, R., Weiner, G. and Willman, C. L. (2022) Leadership Diversity and Development in the Nation's Cancer Centers. Journal of the National Cancer Institute, Vol: 114(9), pp. 1214–1221. https://doi.org/10.1093/jnci/djac121

Levett-Jones, T. and Lathlean, J. (2008) Belongingness: A prerequisite for nursing students' clinical learning. Nurse Education in Practice, Vol: 8(2), pp. 103–111. https://doi.org/10.1016/j.nepr.2007.04.003

Lister, S., Hofland, J. and Grafton, H. and Wilson, C. (Eds.)

(2021) The Royal Marsden Manual of Clinical Nursing Procedures, Student Edition (10th ed.). Chichester: Wiley Blackwell.

Lopez-Gavira, L.G., Moriña, A. and Morgado, B. (2021) Challenges to inclusive education at the university: the perspective of students and disability support service staff. Innovation, Vol: 34(3), pp. 292–304. https://doi.org/10.1080/13511610.2019.1578198

Mallman, M. and Lee, H. (2017) Isolated learners: young mature-age students, university culture, and desire for academic sociality, International Journal of Lifelong Education, Vol: 36(5), pp. 512-525, DOI: 10.1080/02601370.2017.1302012

Manderscheid, A. (2022) Leveraging Student-Centred Learning Through SMART Goals Within Undergraduate Clinical Experiences. Nurse Educator, Publish Ahead of Print. https://doi.org/10.1097/NNE.0000000000001352

McCormack, B., McCance, T., Bulley, C., Brown, D., McMillan, A. and Martin, S. (Eds.) (2021) Fundamentals of Person-Centred Healthcare Practice: A Guide for Healthcare Students. Chichester: Wiley Blackwell.

McKenna, L., Brown, T., Williams, B. and Lau, R. (2020) Empathic and listening styles of first year undergraduate nursing students: A cross-sectional study. Journal of Professional Nursing, Vol: 36(6), pp. 611–615. https://doi.org/10.1016/j.profnurs.2020.08.013

Microsoft (2023) Microsoft 365. [Online] Available: https://www.microsoft.com/en-gb/microsoft-365?ocid=cmmttvzgpuyandrtc=1 [Accessed: 22 July 2023].

Minton, C. and Birks, M. (2019) "You can't escape it": Bullying experiences of New Zealand nursing students on clinical placement. Nurse Education Today, Vol: 77, pp. 12–17. https://doi.org/10.1016/j.nedt.2019.03.002

Molesworth, M. (2017) Nursing students' first placement: Peripherality and marginality within the community of practice. The Journal of Nursing Education, Vol: 56(1), pp. 31–38. https://doi.org/10.3928/01484834-20161219-0

Molesworth, M. and Lewitt, M. (2016) Preregistration nursing students' perspectives on the learning, teaching and application of bioscience knowledge within practice. Journal of Clinical Nursing, Vol: 25(5-6), pp. 725–732. https://doi.org/10.1111/jocn.13020

Moreno-Poyato, A. R. and Rodríguez-Nogueira, Ó. (2021) The association between empathy and the nurse–patient therapeutic relationship in mental health units: a cross-sectional study. Journal of Psychiatric and Mental Health Nursing, Vol: 28(3), pp. 335–343. https://doi.org/10.1111/jpm.12675

Morley, D., Bettles, S. and Derham, C. (2019) The exploration of students' learning gain following immersive simulation - the impact of feedback. Higher Education Pedagogies, Vol: 4(1), pp. 368–384. https://doi.org/10.1080/23752696.2019.1642123

Mudallal, R. H., Othman, W. M. and Al Hassan, N. F. (2017) Nurses' Burnout: The Influence of Leader Empowering Behaviors, Work Conditions, and Demographic Traits. Inquiry. Vol: 54, pp. 1-5.

Nakamura, H., Tawatsuji, Y., Fang, S. and Matsui, T. (2021) Explanation of emotion regulation mechanism of mindfulness using a brain function model. Neural Networks, Vol: 138, pp. 198–214. https://doi.org/10.1016/j.neunet.2021.01.029

National Institute for Health and Care Excellence (2023) NICE guidance. [Online] Available: https://www.nice.org.uk/guidance [Accessed: 01 August 2023].

National Institute for Health and Care Research (2023) About us. [Online] Available: https://www.nihr.ac.uk/about-us/ [Accessed: 03 August 2023].

National Union of Students (2023) About [Online] Available: https://www.nus.org.uk/about [Accessed: 01 August 2023].

NHS Health Careers (2023a) Agenda for Change Pay Rates. [Online] Available: https://www.healthcareers.nhs.uk/working-health/working-nhs/nhs-pay-and-benefits/agenda-change-pay-rates [Accessed: 4 April 2023].

NHS Health Careers (2023b) Nursing Associate. [Online] Available: https://www.healthcareers.nhs.uk/explore-roles/nursing/roles-nursing/nursing-associate [Accessed: 4 April 2023].

NHS Business Services Authority (2022) Financial support for healthcare students 2022/23. [Online] Available: https://www.nhsbsa.nhs.uk/nhs-learning-support-fund-lsf [Accessed: 23 May 2023].

NHS Employers (2020) How to embed flexible working for nurses. London: NHS Confederation.

NHS Employers (2021) Work health assessments. [Online] Available: https://www.nhsemployers.org/system/files/2021-10/Work%20health%20assessments_August%202021.pdf [Accessed: 21 April 2023]

NHS Health Education England (2023) Nursing associates. [Online] Available: https://www.hee.nhs.uk/our-work/nursing-associates [Accessed: 02 May 2023].

NI Direct (2023a) Disclosure and criminal record check. [Online] Available: https://www.nidirect.gov.uk/information-and-services/accessni-criminal-record-checks/apply-accessni-check [Accessed: 14 July 2023].

NI Direct (2023b) Health professional courses. [Online] Available: https://www.nidirect.gov.uk/articles/health-professional-courses [Accessed: 14 July 2023].

Nursing and Midwifery Council (2018a) The Code: Professional standards of practice and behaviour for nurses, midwives and nursing associates [Online] Available: https://www.nmc.org.uk/standards/code/ [Accessed: 21 January 2023].

Nursing and Midwifery Council (2018b) Standards for pre-registration nursing programmes. [Online] Available: https://www.nmc.org.uk/standards/standards-for-nurses/standards-for-pre-registration-nursing-programmes/ [Accessed: 21 November 2022].

Nursing and Midwifery Council (2018c) Future nurse: Standards of proficiency for registered nurses. [Online] Available: https://www.nmc.org.uk/globalassets/sitedocuments/standards-of-proficiency/nurses/future-nurse-proficiencies.pdf [Accessed: 12 March 2023].

Nursing and Midwifery Council (2018d) Enabling professionalism in nursing and midwifery practice. [Online] Available: https://www.nmc.org.uk/standards/guidance/professionalism/read-report/ [Accessed: 22 January 2023].

Nursing and Midwifery Council (2019) Role differences between nursing associates and nurses [Online] Available: https://www.nmc.org.uk/news/news-and-updates/blog-whats-a-nursing-associate/ [Accessed: 21 November 2021].

Nursing and Midwifery Council (2020) Registration and Qualification Codes. [Online] Available: https://www.nmc.org.uk/registration/your-registration/statement-of-entry/registration-and-qualification-codes/ [Accessed: 1 May 2023].

Nursing and Midwifery Council (2021) What is revalidation? [Online] Available: https://www.nmc.org.uk/revalidation/overview/what-is-revalidation/ [Accessed: 14 February 2023]

Nursing and Midwifery Council (2022a) About us. [Online] Available: https://www.nmc.org.uk/about-us/ [Accessed: 14 February 2022].

Nursing and Midwifery Council (2022b) Guidance on using social media responsibly. [Online] Available: https://www.nmc.org.uk/standards/guidance/social-media-guidance/ [Accessed: 22 June 2023].

Nursing and Midwifery Council (2023a) Registration data reports. [Online] Available: https://www.nmc.org.uk/about-us/reports-and-accounts/registration-statistics/ [Accessed: 21 July 2023].

Nursing and Midwifery Council (2023b) Simulated Practice Learning. [Online] Available: https://www.nmc.org.uk/standards/guidance/supporting-information-for-our-education-and-training-standards/simulated-practice-learning/ [Accessed: 5 May 2023].

Nursing and Midwifery Council (2023c) We regulate nursing associates. [Online] Available: https://www.nmc.org.uk/about-us/our-role/who-we-regulate/nursing-associates/ [Accessed: 21 July 2023].

O'Flynn-Magee, K., Rodney, P., Pearson, M., Afonso Burnay, M. and Daly, Z. (2020) Interrupting the cycle of bullying witnessed or experienced by nursing students: An ethical and relational action framework. Nurse Education Today, Vol: 91, 104458–104458. https://doi.org/10.1016/j.nedt.2020.104458

Office for National Statistics (2021) Coronavirus and first year higher education students, England: 4 October to 11 October 2021. [Online] Available: https://www.ons.gov.uk/peoplepopulationandcommunity/healthandsocialcare/healthandwell-being/bulletins/coronavirusandfirstyearhighereducationstudentsengland/4octoberto11october2021 [Accessed: 08 August 2023].

Oliver, D. (2020) Staff hydration matters more than keeping up appearances. BMJ, Vol: 368, pp. 1-2. https://doi.org/10.1136/bmj.l7088

Open University (2023) Nursing and Healthcare courses. [Online] Available: https://www.open.ac.uk/courses/nursing-healthcare [Accessed: 12 August 2023].

Ordu, Y. and Caliskan, N. (2023) The impact of a web-based mind map learning technique on students' nursing knowledge of the nursing process. International Journal of Nursing Knowledge, Vol: 34(2), pp. 108–115. https://doi.org/10.1111/2047-3095.12374

Osakwe, Z. T., Larson, E., Agrawal, M. and Shang, J. (2017) Assessment of Activity of Daily Living Among Older Adult Patients in Home Healthcare and Skilled Nursing Facilities: An Integrative Review. Home Healthcare Now, Vol: 35(5), pp. 258–267. https://doi.org/10.1097/NHH.0000000000000537

Owen, L., Apps, L., Stanulewicz, N., Hall, A. and Laird, K.

(2022) Health care worker knowledge and attitudes towards uniform laundering during the COVID-19 pandemic. American Journal of Infection Control, Vol: 50(5), pp. 525–535. https://doi.org/10.1016/j.ajic.2021.12.017

Patel, S. E., Chrisman, M., Russell, C. L., Lasiter, S., Bennett, K. and Pahls, M. (2022) Cross-sectional study of the relationship between experiences of incivility from staff nurses and undergraduate nursing students' sense of belonging to the nursing profession. Nurse Education in Practice, Vol: 62, pp. 1-7. https://doi.org/10.1016/j.nepr.2022.103320

Paterson, K. and Wallar, J. (2017) Clinical Placements: A Pocket Guide. Banbury: Lantern Publishing.

Pearce, L. (2021) Medicines management: a guide for students: Do you feel daunted by this area of nursing practice? Nursing Standard, Vol: 36(7), pp. 56–57. https://doi.org/10.7748/ns.36.7.56.s24

Pearce, L. (2022) Neurodiverse conditions: learning to study your way: Advice from nursing students with conditions such as dyslexia, dyspraxia and autism on strategies that can help and how to seek support. Nursing Standard, Vol: 37(2), pp. 26–27. https://doi.org/10.7748/ns.37.2.26.s15

Pears, R. and Shields, G. (2022) Cite Them Right: The Essential Referencing Guide (12th ed.). London: Bloomsbury Publishing.

Peate, I. (Ed.) (2019) Alexander's Nursing Practice: Hospital and Home (5th ed.). London: Elsevier.

Pokorny, H., Holley, D. and Kane, S. (2017) Commuting, transitions and belonging: the experiences of students living at home in their first year at university. *High Educ* **74**, pp. 543–558. https://doi.org/10.1007/s10734-016-0063-3

Polyakova-Norwood, V., Creed, J., Patterson, B. and Heiney, S. (2023) Making group work gratifying: Implementing and evaluating a three-stage model of group processes in an online nursing course. Journal of Professional Nursing, Vol: 46, pp. 13–18. https://doi.org/10.1016/j.profnurs.2023.02.004

Pront, L. and McNeill, L. (2019) Nursing students' perceptions of a clinical learning assessment activity: "Linking the puzzle pieces of theory to practice." Nurse Education in Practice, Vol: 36, pp. 85–90. https://doi.org/10.1016/j.nepr.2019.03.008

Pryjmachuk, S., McWilliams, C., Hannity, B., Ellis, J. and Griffiths, J. (2019) Transitioning to university as a nursing student: Thematic analysis of written reflections. Nurse Education Today, Vol: 74, pp. 54–60. https://doi.org/10.1016/j.nedt.2018.12.003

QS World University Rankings (2023) University Rankings. [Online] Available: https://www.topuniversities.com/university-rankings [Accessed: 03 July 2023].

Quality Assurance Agency for Higher Education (2021) What is Credit? A guide for students. [Online] Available: https://www.qaa.ac.uk/docs/qaa/quality-code/what-is-credit-guide-for-students.pdf [Accessed: 07 June 2023].

Razik, R. A. A., Abdalla, E. S., Ali, H. H. and Mahmoud, S. F. (2021) Relation between level of depressive symptoms and self assertiveness among nursing students. Annals of the Romanian Society for Cell Biology, Vol: 25(3), pp. 5073–5088.

RCN Foundation (2023) Financial support for undergraduate nursing and midwifery students [Online] Available: https://rcnfoundation.rcn.org.uk/Grants-and-funding/Hardship-grants/financial-support-for-undergraduates [Accessed: 03 August 2023].

Rees, C. and Monrouxe, L. (2016) Student life - Cause for concern: What do you do if you see a nurse giving poor care? A subtle response can be effective, say two experts. Nursing Standard, Vol: 30(22), p. 66. https://doi.org/10.7748/ns.30.22.66.s52

Royal College of Nursing (2019) Mindful moments on the move. [Online] Available: https://www.rcn.org.uk/magazines/bulletin/2019/june/mindfulness-meditation-tools-june-2019 [Accessed: 02 May 2023].

Royal College of Nursing (2022a) Investing in Patient Safety and Outcomes. [Online] Available: https://www.rcn.org.uk/Professional-Development/publications/investing-in-patient-safety-and-outcomes-uk-pub-010-567 [Accessed: 04 April 2023].

Royal College of Nursing (2022b) 10 reasons to support strike action. [Online] Available: https://www.rcn.org.uk/magazines/Action/2022/Oct/10-reasons-to-vote-for-strike-action [Accessed: 22 February 2023].

Royal College of Nursing (2023a) About the RCN. [Online] Available: https://www.rcn.org.uk/about-us [Accessed: 01 August 2023].

Royal College of Nursing (2023b) Prioritising personal safety. [Online] Available: https://www.rcn.org.uk/Get-Help/RCN-advice/prioritising-personal-safety [Accessed: 01 August 2023].

Royal College of Nursing (2023c) Conflicts of Interest. [Online] Available: https://www.rcn.org.uk/Get-Help/RCN-advice/nursing-staff-and-potential-conflict-of-interest [Accessed: 03 August 2023].

Salamonson, Y., Priddis, H., Woodmass, J. M., Everett, B., Lynch, J., Curtis, E. and Ramjan, L. M. (2018) The price of journeying towards the prize—Commencing nursing students' experiences of working and studying: A qualitative study. Journal of Clinical Nursing, Vol: 27(21-22), pp. 4141–4149. https://doi.org/10.1111/jocn.14583

Salamonson, Y., Roach, D., Crawford, R., McGrath, B., Christiansen, A., Wall, P., Kelly, M. and Ramjan, L. M. (2020) The type and amount of paid work while studying influence academic performance of first year nursing students: An inception cohort study. Nurse Education Today, Vol: 84, 104213–104213. https://doi.org/10.1016/j.nedt.2019.104213

Scottish Government (2022) Paramedic, nursing and midwifery student support: 2022 to 2023. [Online] Available: https://www.gov.scot/publications/support-paramedic-nursing-midwifery-students-scotland-2022-23/pages/4/ [Accessed: 10 July 2023].

Scottish Government (2023) Criminal records check. [Online] Available: https://www.mygov.scot/browse/working-jobs/finding-a-job/disclosure [Accessed: 14 July 2023].

Scottish Intercollegiate Guidelines Network (2023) SIGN makes sense of evidence. [Online] Available: https://www.sign.ac.uk/ [Accessed: 01 August 2023].

Sensenig, J. (2022) Learning through practice. Nursing, Vol: 52(4), pp. 46-50. doi: 10.1097/01.NURSE.0000823288.86932.46

Septiani, W. E., Sulistyaningsih, S. and Syakur, A. (2022) The Effectiveness of Pomodoro Technique on Students' Descriptive Text Writing Quality. Jurnal Basicedu (Online), Vol: 6(3), pp. 3384–3390. https://doi.org/10.31004/basicedu.v6i3.2619

Sheerin, F. and Curtis, E. A. (2019) Leadership for Intellectual Disability Service: Motivating Change and Improvement.

Abingdon: Routledge. https://doi.org/10.4324/9781351172400.

Siviter, B. (2013) The Student Nurse Handbook (3rd ed.). London: Elsevier.

Smith, L., Disler, R. and Watson, K. (2020) Physical activity and dietary habits of first year nursing students: An Australian dual-method study. Collegian (Royal College of Nursing, Australia), Vol: 27(5), pp. 535–541. https://doi.org/10.1016/j.colegn.2020.05.002

Snowden, A., Stenhouse, R., Young, J., Carver, H., Carver, F. and Brown, N. (2015) The relationship between emotional intelligence, previous caring experience and mindfulness in student nurses and midwives: a cross sectional analysis. Nurse Education Today, 35(1), pp. 152–158. https://doi.org/10.1016/j.nedt.2014.09.004

Social Care Institute for Excellence (2020) Privacy and dignity in care. [Online] Available: https://www.scie.org.uk/dignity/care/privacy [Accessed: 05 July 2023].

Stacey, P. (2022) 5 Tips For Disabled Students Starting University [Online] Available: https://www.accessable.co.uk/articles/5-tips-for-disabled-students-starting-university [Accessed: 07 June 2023].

Stevens, J. A. (2011) Student nurses' career preferences for working with older people: A replicated longitudinal survey. International Journal of Nursing Studies, Vol: 48(8), pp. 944–951. https://doi.org/10.1016/j.ijnurstu.2011.01.004

Stevens, N., McNiesh, S. and Goyal, D. (2020) Utilizing an SBAR Workshop with Baccalaureate Nursing Students to Improve Communication Skills. Nursing Education Perspectives, Vol: 41(2), pp. 117–118.

https://doi.org/10.1097/01.NEP.0000000000000518

Student Information Scotland (2020) Your guide to freshers' week. [Online] Available: https://www.studentinformation.gov.scot/students/student-life/freshers-week [Accessed: 12 February 2023].

Student Loans Company (2023) [Online] Available: https://www.gov.uk/government/news/student-loans-company-reminds-new-students-to-apply-now [Accessed: 18 May 2023]

Sundling, V., Sundler, A. J., Holmström, I. K., Kristensen, D. V. and Eide, H. (2017) Mindfulness predicts student nurses' communication self-efficacy: A cross-national comparative study. Patient Education and Counseling, Vol: 100(8), pp. 1558–1563. https://doi.org/10.1016/j.pec.2017.03.016

The King's Fund (2020) The courage of compassion. [Online] Available: https://www.kingsfund.org.uk/publications/courage-compassion-supporting-nurses-midwives [Accessed: 15 May 2023]

Thompson, D. (2019) Staying Well and Safe at University. London: Trigger Publishing

Thompson, G. N., McClement, S. E., Peters, S., Hack, T. F., Chochinov, H. and Funk, L. (2021) More than just a task: intimate care delivery in the nursing home. International Journal of Qualitative Studies on Health and Well-Being, Vol: 16(1), pp. 1-10. https://doi.org/10.1080/17482631.2021.1943123

Thomson, A. E., Smith, N. and Karpa, J. (2023) Teaching Professional Boundaries in Psychiatric Nursing: Resource Development. The Journal of Nursing Education, Vol: 62(2), pp. 97–100. https://doi.org/10.3928/01484834-20221213-05

Times Higher Education (2023) World University Rankings 2023

[Online] Available: https://www.timeshighereducation.com/world-university-rankings/2023/world-ranking [Accessed: 03 July 2023].

UCAS (2023a) What is Clearing. [Online] Available: https://www.ucas.com/undergraduate/applying-university/writing-personal-statement/how-write-personal-statement [Accessed: 1 June 2023].

UCAS (2023b) How to write your undergraduate personal statement. [Online] Available: https://www.ucas.com/undergraduate/clearing-and-results-day/what-clearing [Accessed: 1 June 2023].

UCAS (2023c) Personal Statement Worksheet [Online] Available: https://www.ucas.com/sites/default/files/ucas-personal-statement-worksheet.pdf [Accessed: 07 July 2023].

UCAS (2023d) Writing your personal statement [Online] Available: https://www.ucas.com/undergraduate/applying-university/writing-your-personal-statement [Accessed: 07 July 2023].

UCAS (2023e) Scholarships, grants, and bursaries [Online] Available: https://www.ucas.com/finance/scholarships-grants-and-bursaries [Accessed: 03 August 2023].

UCAS (2023f) How to get support from your universities and colleges [Online] Available: https://www.ucas.com/undergraduate/student-life/how-get-support-your-universities-and-colleges [Accessed: 07 August 2023].

UK Government (2023a) Disclosure and Barring Service. [Online] Available: https://www.gov.uk/government/organisations/disclosure-and-barring-service [Accessed: 02 June 2023].

UK Government (2023b) Repaying your student loan. [Online] Available: https://www.gov.uk/repaying-your-student-loan [Accessed: 12 June 2023].

UK Government (2023c) Student finance for undergraduate. [Online] Available: https://www.gov.uk/student-finance/new-fulltime-students [Accessed: 02 June 2023].

UK Government (2023d) Extra money to pay for university. [Online] Available: https://www.gov.uk/extra-money-pay-university/university-and-college-hardship-funds [Accessed: 12 June 2023].

UK Government (2023e) Universal Credit. [Online] Available: https://www.gov.uk/universal-credit [Accessed: 12 June 2023].

UK Parliament (2023) Student mental health in England: Statistics policy and guidance. [Online] Available: https://commonslibrary.parliament.uk/research-briefings/cbp-8593/ [Accessed: 08 August 2023].

University of Oxford (2023) Essay and dissertation writing skills. [Online] Available: https://www.ox.ac.uk/students/academic/guidance/skills/essay [Accessed: 10 June 2023].

van der Riet, P., Levett-Jones, T. and Aquino-Russell, C. (2018) The effectiveness of mindfulness meditation for nurses and nursing students: An integrated literature review. Nurse Education Today, Vol: 65, pp. 201–211. https://doi.org/10.1016/j.nedt.2018.03.018

Vescovelli, F., Melani, P., Ruini, C., Ricci Bitti, P. E. and Monti, F. (2017) University Counseling Service for Improving Students' Mental Health. Psychological Services, Vol: 14(4), pp. 470–480.

https://doi.org/10.1037/ser0000166

Walker, B. W. (2022) Tackling the personal tutoring conundrum: A qualitative study on the impact of developmental support for tutors. Active Learning in Higher Education, Vol: 23(1), 65–77. https://doi.org/10.1177/1469787420926007

Watson, C. (2018) The language of kindness. A nurse's story. London: Chatto and Windus.

Waugh, A. and Grant, A. (2018) Ross and Wilson Anatomy and Physiology in Health and Illness (14th Ed) London: Elsevier.

Westerdahl, F., Carlson, E., Wennick, A. and Borglin, G. (2020) Teaching strategies and outcome assessments targeting critical thinking in bachelor nursing students: a scoping review protocol. BMJ Open, Vol: 10(1), pp. 11-6. https://doi.org/10.1136/bmjopen-2019-033214

White, S., Stainer, L., Cooper, K. and Waight, S. (2018) The personal tutor as a role model for students: humanising nursing care. British Journal of Nursing (Mark Allen Publishing), Vol: 27(1), pp. 52–55. https://doi.org/10.12968/bjon.2018.27.1.52

Williams, C. A. (2020) Nursing Students' Mindsets Matter: Cultivating a Growth Mindset. Nurse Educator, Vol: 45(5), pp. 252–256. https://doi.org/10.1097/NNE.0000000000000798

Wirth, M. D., Meyer, J., Jessup, A. and Dawson, R. M. (2023) Barriers and Facilitators of Diet, Physical Activity Levels, and Sleep Among Nursing Undergraduates and Early-Career Nurses: A Qualitative Descriptive Study. American Journal of Health Promotion, 37(6), pp. 821–829. https://doi.org/10.1177/08901171231179437

Wise, Y., Ossenberg, C. and Henderson, A. (2022) The

contribution of paid employment for students during their pre-registration nursing studies: An integrative review. Nurse Education Today, Vol: 111, 105296–105296. https://doi.org/10.1016/j.nedt.2022.105296

Wong, F. M. F., Kan, C. W. Y. and Chow, S. K. Y. (2022) From resistance to acceptance in small group work: Students' narratives. Nurse Education Today, Vol: 111, pp. 1-6. https://doi.org/10.1016/j.nedt.2022.105317

World Health Organisation (2009) Your 5 Moments for Hand Hygiene. [Online] Available: https://www.who.int/multi-media/details/your-5-moments-for-hand-hygiene-poster [Accessed: 23 June 2023].

ABOUT THE AUTHOR

Mark is a Registered Nurse and Senior Lecturer based in Scotland. He has a wealth of experience within a variety of care settings, including nursing roles in the Royal Air Force, Scottish Prison Service and acute NHS services. He is passionate about nurse education and supporting students in developing the knowledge required to underpin successful careers in nursing. Mark is the Programme Lead at a large Scottish University for BSc/BSc (Hons) Nursing Studies across all four fields of nursing. He enjoys supporting students in linking theory and practice. His PhD explored student nurses' experiences of the social sciences and biosciences during their studies. Mark is married with three children and a pet dog. He enjoys family camping trips to Cornwall.

Printed in Great Britain
by Amazon

27656578R00139